Business Tax

(Finance Act 2014)

Workbook

for assessments from January 2015

Aubrey Penning
Bob Thomas

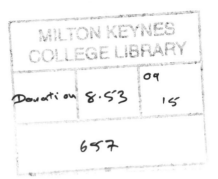
Published by Osborne Books Limited
Unit 1B Everoak Estate
Bromyard Road, Worcester WR2 5HP
Tel 01905 748071
Email books@osbornebooks.co.uk
Website www.osbornebooks.co.uk

Design by Laura Ingham

Printed by CPI Group (UK) Limited, Croydon, CR0 4YY, on environmentally friendly, acid-free paper from managed forests.

MIX
Paper from
responsible sources
FSC® C013604

British Library Cataloguing in Publication Data
A catalogue record for this book is available from the British Library

ISBN 978 1909173 484

Contents

Introduction

Chapter activities

Chapter activities – answers

Practice assessments – tasks

Practice assessments – answers

Acknowledgements

The publisher wishes to thank the following for their help with the reading and production of the book: Jon Moore, Bee Pugh and Cathy Turner. Thanks are also due to Laura Ingham for her designs for this series.

The publisher is indebted to the Association of Accounting Technicians for its help and advice to our author and editor during the preparation of this text.

Author and Technical Editor

Aubrey Penning has many years experience of teaching accountancy on a variety of courses in Worcester and Gwent. He is a Certified Accountant, and before his move into full-time teaching he worked for the health service, a housing association and a chemical supplier. For many years he was the AAT course coordinator at Worcester College of Technology, specialising in the areas of management accounting and taxation.

Bob Thomas, the Technical Editor of this book, has been involved with the Education and Training activities of the AAT since 1986, including the development and piloting of the skills-based scheme. He is an external verifier, a simulation writer, a moderator and a contributor at workshops, training days, conferences and master classes. Until recently he was a member of the Learning and Development Board and Chairman of the Assessment Panel.

Introduction

what this book covers

This book has been written to cover the 'Business tax' Unit which is an optional Unit for the revised (2013) AAT Level 4 Diploma in Accounting.

what this book contains

This book is set out in two sections:

- **Chapter Activities** which provide extra practice material in addition to the activities included in the Osborne Books Tutorial text. Answers to the Chapter activities are included in this book.

- **Practice Assessments** are provided to prepare the student for the computer-based assessments. They are based directly on the structure, style and content of the sample assessment material provided by the AAT at www.aat.org.uk. Suggested answers to the Practice Assessments are set out in this book.

further information

If you want to know more about our products and resources, please visit www.osbornebooks.co.uk for further details and access to our online shop.

Chapter activities

1 Introduction to business taxation

1.1 Which of the following statements are correct? ✔

	True	False
(a) A self employed taxpayer must pay Class 2 NIC, unless the 'small earnings exception' is claimed		
(b) Class 4 NIC is payable by the self employed only when drawings are over £7,956		
(c) Class 4 NIC is payable by the self employed when profits are over £7,956		
(d) Class 4 NIC is paid throughout the tax year		
(e) Class 4 NIC is payable at 2% on profits over £41,865		

1.2 Using the following table, insert the details and dates relating to online returns and payment of tax

	Period return relates to	Latest return submission date	Latest tax payment date
Corporation Tax			
Income Tax			

Select from the following:

- Tax year
- Financial year
- 12 months after end of tax year
- 12 months after end of chargeable accounting period
- 9 months and one day after end of chargeable accounting period
- 12 months after end of period that accounts are based on
- Chargeable accounting period
- 31 January following tax year
- 31 October following tax year

1.3

(1)   A taxpayer has self employed income of £60,000 for the tax year 2014/15. The amount chargeable to NIC at 9% would be

£ _____

(2)   A taxpayer has self employed income of £45,000 for the tax year 2014/15. The amount of total Class 4 NIC payable would be

£ _____

1.4   State whether each of the following is true or false.

		True	False
(a)	A self employed individual's tax records relating to his business for 2014/15 need to be kept until 31 January 2021, or longer if an investigation is being carried out		
(b)	HMRC has a right to visit premises to inspect records		
(c)	Accountants must normally follow the rules of confidentiality, but there are exceptions		
(d)	Where a practitioner has knowledge or suspicion that his client is money laundering, then he has a duty to inform the relevant person or authority		
(e)	The AAT Code of Professional Ethics applies to AAT members, but not to AAT students		
(f)	When an accountant is advising a client the greatest duty of care is to HMRC		

1.5   State the final submission dates for tax returns for the following businesses.

A sole trader with accounts made up to 31 March 2015.	
A sole trader with accounts made up to 30 June 2015.	
A limited company with accounts made up to 31 December 2014.	

2   Corporation tax – trading profits

2.1   A limited company has the income and expenses as shown in the following table recorded in its statement of profit or loss. In order to calculate the adjusted trading profit, some items need to be added and some deducted from the net profit. Some items do not require any adjustment.

Analyse the income and expenses, by ticking the appropriate columns in the table.

✔

	Add to net profit	Deduct from net profit	No adjustment required
Depreciation			
Discount received			
Directors' salaries			
Dividends received			
Rent receivable			
Rent payable			
Interest payable			
Advertising costs			
Entertaining customers			

2.2 River Limited has the following summarised statement of profit or loss.

	£	£
Sales		120,000
less cost of sales		35,000
gross profit		85,000
add gain on sale of non-current asset		12,000
		97,000
less expenses:		
administration expenses	18,000	
depreciation	13,000	
charitable payments (gift-aid)	2,000	
entertaining staff	5,000	
vehicle expenses	22,000	
		60,000
Net profit		37,000

Select the adjusted trading profit (before capital allowances) from the following.

		✔
(a)	£57,000	
(b)	£45,000	
(c)	£40,000	
(d)	£34,000	
(e)	£37,000	
(f)	£38,000	

2.3 State whether the following statements are true or false. ✔

	True	False
(a) The basis of assessment for trading profits is the tax adjusted trading profits of the chargeable accounting period, prepared on an accruals basis		
(b) Lease rental payments for cars are never allowable as they are deemed to be capital expenditure		
(c) Interest payable on trade loans is not allowable		
(d) If a loan to an employee is written off the amount is not an allowable deduction		
(e) Donations to political parties are an allowable expense		
(f) Employers' national insurance contributions are not an allowable deduction as they are effectively a form of taxation		
(g) Employees' parking fines incurred while on business are an allowable deduction		

2.4 If an accounting period is longer than 12 months, which of the following statements shows the correct approach?

✔

(a) Provided the accounting period is not more than 18 months long, the whole period can form one chargeable accounting period	
(b) The capital allowances are calculated for the long accounting period and deducted from the adjusted trading profits for the long accounting period. This is then time-apportioned into two chargeable accounting periods	
(c) It is illegal to prepare accounts for a limited company for more than 12 months, so the problem does not arise	
(d) The trading profits for the long accounting period are time-apportioned into two periods before tax adjustments are carried out to each period's profit. Capital allowances are calculated for the long period and then time-apportioned, before being deducted from each period's adjusted profits	
(e) The trading profits for the long period are adjusted for tax purposes (before capital allowances), and the result is time-apportioned into two chargeable accounting periods. Separate capital allowance computations are carried out for each chargeable accounting period, and then deducted from each of the adjusted trading profits	

2.5   A limited company has the following tax-adjusted results for years to 31 December 2013 and 2014:

	2013	2014
Trading Income	£50,000	£0
Income from Investments	£18,000	£15,000
Chargeable Gains	£0	£10,000

The company made a trading loss in 2014 of £81,000.

What is the maximum amount of loss that could be set against the taxable total profits for 2013?

		✔
(a)	£56,000	
(b)	£68,000	
(c)	£50,000	
(d)	£66,000	
(e)	£0	

3 Corporation tax – capital allowances

3.1 Analyse the following items into those that qualify as plant and machinery for capital allowance purposes, (under corporation tax) and those that do not, by ticking the appropriate column.

	Qualifying	Not qualifying
Car for employee's private use		
Office furniture		
Capital expenditure on software		
Payments for vehicle on operating lease		
Vehicles bought on credit		
Buildings		
Equipment bought through hire purchase		

3.2 A company has a 12-month chargeable accounting period ending on 31/3/2015, with no written down values brought forward for capital allowance purposes. During the period the company purchased:

- A new low-emission car for £26,000
- A car with emissions of 180 g/km for £22,000
- Plant for £60,000

Calculate the maximum capital allowances that can be claimed, and insert the figures into the following sentences.

The AIA that can be claimed is £

The first year allowance that can be claimed at 100% is £

The writing down allowance that can be claimed at 18% is £

The writing down allowance that can be claimed at 8% is £

The total capital allowance that can be claimed is £

3.3 Analyse each of the following capital acquisitions into the relevant category by ticking the appropriate column.

✔

	AIA (to limit)	Main Pool	Special Rate Pool	100% FYA
Car emissions of 185 g/km				
Car emissions of 99 g/km				
Machinery				
Zero-emission goods vehicle				
Car emissions of 125 g/km				
Water-efficient plant				

3.4 State whether the following statements are true or false.

✔

	True	False
(a) For a CAP of 9 months, the AIA for each acquisition that qualifies would be scaled down to 9/12 of its cost. For example, an asset bought for £20,000 would only be entitled to £15,000 AIA		
(b) For a CAP of 9 months any writing down allowance would be scaled down to 9/12 of the equivalent amount for a 12 month period, but first year allowances and balancing allowances would not be affected		
(c) For a CAP of 9 months any first year allowance would be scaled down to 9/12 of the equivalent amount for a 12 month period, but writing down allowances and balancing allowances would not be affected		
(d) For a CAP of 9 months the annual investment allowance (AIA) limit would be calculated by time-apportionment		
(e) For a CAP of 9 months the writing down allowance is unaffected		

3.5   A company has the following information regarding its non-current assets for a 12-month CAP, ending on 31/12/2014.

	£
Written down values brought forward:	
General (main) pool	120,000
Special rate pool	19,000
Additions:	
Machinery (purchased January 2014)	60,000
New car for Sales Director (emissions 190 g/km)	35,000
Disposals:	
Machinery	5,000
Sales Director's car (special rate pool)	7,000

Calculate the maximum capital allowances for the CAP.

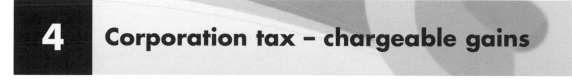

4   Corporation tax – chargeable gains

4.1   Select the appropriate disposal proceeds amount to be used in the chargeable gains computation of a limited company by ticking the appropriate column.

✔

	Actual Proceeds	Market Value	£6,000	Zero
Sale of asset for £15,000 to Director who owns 80% of shares in company. Market value of asset is £35,000				
Gift of asset to unconnected individual (non-shareholder)				
Sale of asset to company employee (non-shareholder) at below market value				
Sale of chattel for £4,000 (its market value) that had originally cost £10,000				
Destruction of an uninsured asset during fire				
Sale of asset for £15,000 to Director who owns 10% of shares in company. Market value of asset is £35,000				
Shares owned in an unconnected company that have become worthless due to the company's liquidation				

4.2   Tousist Ltd sold an antique office desk for £10,000 in April 2014. This was bought for £3,500 in August 2000. The indexation factor from August 2000 to April 2014 was 0.500.

Complete the following computation:

Proceeds   £

Cost   £

Indexation allowance   £

Gain   £

Chattel restriction on gain   £

State whether the chattel restriction will have any effect on the original gain.   YES / NO

4.3   Penfold Ltd bought 8,000 shares in Tempter Ltd for £19,500 in October 2001. A rights issue of 1 for 40 shares was bought in July 2003 for £1.80 per share. In April 2014, Penfold Ltd sold 6,000 of the shares for £4 per share.

Indexation factors were: October 2001 to July 2003: 0.114; July 2003 to April 2014: 0.410

What is the gain made on the share disposal?

	No. Shares	Cost £	Indexed Cost £

Proceeds	£
Indexed Cost	£
Gain	£

4.4   Treacle Ltd sold a 2 acre plot of land for £40,000 in April 2014. This was part of a 6 acre plot that was bought for £90,000 in August 2000. The 4 acres that were retained were valued at £60,000 at the time of the sale. The indexation factor from August 2000 to April 2014 was 0.500.

Complete the following computation:

Proceeds   £

Cost   £

Indexation allowance (before restriction)   £

Gain or (Loss)   £

4.5   Trapper Ltd sold a painting for £5,500 in April 2014. This was bought for £7,500 in August 2000. The indexation factor from August 2000 to April 2014 was 0.500.

Complete the following computation:

Proceeds   £

Cost   £

Indexation allowance   £

Gain or (Loss)   £

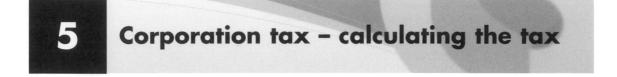

5   Corporation tax – calculating the tax

5.1   Exe Limited is a trading company with no associated companies. For the year ended 31/3/2015 it had the following tax adjusted results:

	£
Trading Profits	600,000
Rental Income	100,000
Dividends Received	45,000

Calculate the corporation tax, using the following table.

	£
Corporation Tax at Main Rate	
Marginal Relief	
Corporation Tax Payable	

5.2   Wye Ltd is a trading company with one associated company. It has the following results for the 8 month CAP to 31/12/2014.

	£
Trading Profits	330,000
Chargeable Gains	40,000
Gift Aid Payments	10,000

Calculate the corporation tax, using the following table.

	£
Maximum of Band	
Corporation Tax at Main Rate	
Marginal Relief	
Corporation Tax Payable	

5.3 Different types of losses can be relieved in different ways. From the list below, select one rule that can apply to each of the losses stated in the table.

Loss	Rules that can apply
Trading Loss	
Capital Loss	
Rental Loss	

Select from:

(a) Set against current period taxable total profits (TTP), with any unused amount carried forward and set against future taxable total profits (TTP)

(b) Set against chargeable gains of same CAP, with any unused loss set against taxable total profits (TTP) of current period

(c) Set against chargeable gains of same CAP, with any unused loss set against chargeable gains of previous period

(d) Set against current period taxable total profits (TTP), with any unused amount carried forward and set against future chargeable gains

(e) Set against trading profits of following CAP

(f) Set against chargeable gains of same CAP, with any unused loss set against chargeable gains of following period

5.4 Xenopus Limited has the following results for the year ended 31/3/2015:

Trading Profits	£1,350,000
Rental Income	£250,000
Chargeable Gains	£220,000
Dividends Received	£180,000

The company also has the following losses brought forward from the previous CAP:

Trade Losses	£ 130,000
Capital Losses	£50,000

Xenopus Limited does not have any associated companies.

Complete page 2 of the short CT600 Corporation Tax Return for Xenopus Limited, including the tax calculation.

A blank form is shown opposite.

Page 2

Company tax calculation

Turnover

1	Total turnover from trade or profession	**1** £

Income

3	Trading and professional profits	**3** £
4	Trading losses brought forward claimed against profits	**4** £
5	Net trading and professional profits	box 3 minus box 4 **5** £
6	Bank, building society or other interest, and profits and gains from non-trading loan relationships	**6** £
11	Income from UK land and buildings	**11** £
14	Annual profits and gains not falling under any other heading	**14** £

Chargeable gains

16	Gross chargeable gains	**16** £
17	Allowable losses including losses brought forward	**17** £
18	Net chargeable gains	box 16 minus box 17 **18** £
21	**Profits before other deductions and reliefs**	sum of boxes 5, 6, 11, 14 & 18 **21** £

Deductions and Reliefs

24	Management expenses under S75 ICTA 1988	**24** £
30	Trading losses of this or a later accounting period under S393A ICTA 1988	**30** £
31	Put an 'X' in box 31 if amounts carried back from later accounting periods are included in box 30	**31**
32	Non-trade capital allowances	**32** £
35	Charges paid	**35** £
37	**Profits chargeable to corporation tax**	box 21 minus boxes 24, 30, 32 and 35 **37** £

Tax calculation

38	Franked investment income	**38** £
39	Number of associated companies in this period or	**39**
40	Associated companies in the first financial year	**40**
41	Associated companies in the second financial year	**41**
42	Put an 'X' in box 42 if the company claims to be charged at the starting rate or the small companies' rate on any part of its profits, or is claiming marginal rate relief	**42**

Enter how much profit has to be charged and at what rate of tax

Financial year (yyyy)	Amount of profit	Rate of tax	Tax	
43	**44** £	**45**	**46** £	p
53	**54** £	**55**	**56** £	p

		total of boxes 46 and 56 **63** £	p
63	Corporation tax		
64	Marginal rate relief	**64** £	p
65	Corporation tax net of marginal rate relief	**65** £	p
66	Underlying rate of corporation tax	**66** • %	
67	Profits matched with non-corporate distributions	**67**	
68	Tax at non-corporate distributions rate	**68** £	p
69	Tax at underlying rate on remaining profits	**69** £	p
70	**Corporation tax chargeable**	See note for box 70 in CT600 Guide **70** £	p

CT600 (Short) (2008) Version 2

5.5   State whether the following statements are true or false.   ✔

		True	False
(a)	Companies must inform HMRC within 6 months that they have started trading. The penalty for failing to notify is £3,000		
(b)	The flat penalty for failure to submit a Corporation Tax Return on time is £100 for up to 3 months late and £200 for over three months late. A percentage penalty based on the Corporation Tax can also apply		
(c)	Interest is charged on late payments (including instalments). The interest charged is an allowable deduction against non-trading interest		
(d)	Errors in tax returns caused by a lack of reasonable care can suffer a penalty of between 0% and 50% of the extra tax due		
(e)	Failure to keep records can result in a penalty of £3,000 per chargeable accounting period		
(f)	Errors in tax returns that are both deliberate and concealed are subject to a penalty of up to 100% of the extra tax due		
(g)	Records need to be kept for at least 6 years from the end of the accounting period		

6 Income tax – trading profits

6.1 From the following factors, tick those that are considered the 'badges of trade' which are used to determine whether an individual is trading.

	✔ Badges of Trade
Reason for acquisition and sale of item(s)	
Whether individual enjoys carrying out the activity	
Whether there is a profit motive	
How long the individual has owned the item(s) before sale	
Whether the individual only sells via computer sites	
Whether any supplementary work is carried out on the item(s) before sale	
Whether the individual considers the activity to be his hobby	
How often the individual carries out similar transactions	
Whether the items bought and sold (the subject matter) are used personally by the individual before sale	

6.2 Analyse the following expenditure of a sole trader into those that are allowable deductions for tax purposes and those that are not, by ticking the appropriate column.

	✔ Allowable expenditure	Non-allowable expenditure
Cost of sales		
Entertaining staff		
Fines for lawbreaking by business owner		
Gifts of food or drink to customers		
Trade bad debts written off		
Salary and NIC of business owner		
Depreciation		
Loss on sale of non-current assets		

6.3 Laura Little is a sole trader. Her business has the following statement of profit or loss:

	£	£
Turnover		1,256,000
Cost of sales		815,400
Gross profit		440,600
Wages and salaries	120,560	
Rent, rates and insurance	51,210	
Repairs to plant	8,615	
Advertising and entertaining	19,535	
Accountancy and legal costs	5,860	
Motor expenses	50,030	
Telephone and office costs	18,050	
Depreciation	22,020	
Other expenses	32,410	328,290
Net Profit		112,310

Notes:

1. Laura took goods from the business that cost £1,200 and would normally sell for £2,000. The cost is included in cost of sales.

2. Wages and salaries include:

	£
Laura Little	45,000
Laura's son, who works during the school holidays	28,000

3. Advertising and entertaining includes:

	£
Gifts to customers:	
Bottles of wine costing £12 each	2,400
400 mouse mats carrying the business's logo	600

4. Motor expenses include:

	£
Delivery van expenses	10,150
Laura's car expenses (used for business only)	5,900
Laura's son's car expenses (used only for private use)	3,800

5. Other expenses include:

	£
Cost of staff training	3,150
Increase in general bad debt provision	2,600

6. Capital allowances have already been calculated at £10,400

Complete the adjusted trading profits computation.

6.4   Mavis Deacon has a 12-month accounting period ending on 30/9/2014, with no written down values brought forward for capital allowance purposes. In January 2014 she purchased:

- A van with 20% private use for £18,000
- A car with emissions of 120 g/km and 40% private use for £20,000
- Machinery for £30,000

Calculate the maximum capital allowances that can be claimed, and insert the figures into the following sentences.

The AIA that can be claimed is   £

The single asset pool writing down allowance that can be claimed is   £

The special rate pool writing down allowance that can be claimed is   £

The total capital allowance that can be claimed is   £

The total written down value carried forward is   £

6.5   A sole trader has the following tax-adjusted results for the tax years 2013/14 and 2014/15:

	2013/14	**2014/15**
Trading Profits	£20,000	£0
Other Income	£17,000	£28,000

The sole trader incurred a trading loss in 2014/15 of £44,000.

What is the maximum amount of the loss that could be set against the individual's income for 2013/14?

	✔
(a) £20,000	
(b) £37,000	
(c) £44,000	
(d) £16,000	
(e) £0	

7   Income tax – further issues

7.1   Clive started trading on 1 November 2012. He makes up his accounts to 31 December each year. The profits were calculated at:

	£
Period to 31 December 2012	16,000
Year to 31 December 2013	108,000
Year to 31 December 2014	92,000

(a)   The tax year in which he started trading was (select one):

2010/11; 2011/12; 2012/13; 2013/14

(b)   His taxable profits in his first tax year of trading were (select one):

£16,000; £43,000; £108,000; £124,000

(c)   His taxable profits in his second tax year of trading were (select one):

£92,000; £97,000; £108,000; £124,000

(d)   His taxable profits in his third tax year of trading were (select one):

£108,000; £124,000; £104,000; £92,000

(e)   His overlap profits were   £

(f)   His overlap profits are deducted (select one):

✔

from his first year profits.	
from the profits in the second year of trading.	
from the profits in the third year of trading.	
from the profits in the final year of trading.	

7.2 An individual commences business as a sole trader on 1 February 2013. He makes his first set of accounts up to 30 April 2014, and thereafter to 30 April each year.

What is the basis period for the tax year 2013/14?

		✔
(a)	1 February 2013 to 30 April 2014	
(b)	1 May 2013 to 30 April 2014	
(c)	1 February 2013 to 31 January 2014	
(d)	6 April 2013 to 5 April 2014	
(e)	1 February 2013 to 5 April 2013	
(f)	1 February 2013 to 5 April 2014	

7.3 Pete and Heather have been in partnership for many years, running a fish smoking business, and sharing profits equally. They have always made their accounts up to 31 December each year.

On 1 September 2014, Ash joined the partnership and the profit sharing ratio was changed to 3:3:2 for Pete, Heather and Ash.

For the year ended 31 December 2014, the trading profit was £120,000.

(1) Using the following table, calculate the division of profits between the partners for the accounting year ended 31 December 2014.

	Total £	Pete £	Heather £	Ash £
1 Jan - 31 August 2014				
1 Sep - 31 Dec 2014				
Total				

(2) What is the basis of assessment for 2014/15 for Ash?

		✔
(a)	1/9/2014 - 31/12/2014	
(b)	1/1/2014 - 31/12/2014	
(c)	1/9/2014 - 5/4/2015	
(d)	1/1/2015 - 5/4/2015	

7.4 Joe Salt's total income tax and Class 4 NIC for 2013/14 has been finalised as £11,600, all relating to his business as a sole trader. He made payments on account of £4,000 on each of 31 January 2014 and 31 July 2014 relating to 2013/14.

Using the following table, calculate the amounts of the payments that he needs to make on 31 January 2015 and 31 July 2015, assuming no claim to reduce payments is made.

		£
Payment on 31 January 2015	Balance of tax and NIC for 2013/14	
	Payment on account for 2014/15	
	Total	
Payment on 31 July 2015	Payment on account for 2014/15	

7.5 Deborah Baker commenced in business on 1 October 2014. She produced accounts for the year ended 30 September 2015, and the information from these accounts has been entered on the self-employment (full) pages (before tax adjustments).

The following items are included in the expenses shown in her accounts:

- Wages and salaries includes her drawings of £20,000

- Telephone costs include £400 for private calls

- Bank charges include £530 interest on her credit card which is for personal use

- Advertising includes entertaining customers costing £1,600, and a staff party costing £450

Deborah has also spent £29,000 on equipment and wishes to claim the maximum Annual Investment Allowance.

Required:

Complete, as far as possible, the remainder of pages 1 to 3 of the full self employment supplementary pages that follow. (The 2013/14 form has been used as the 2014/15 version was not available when this book was published.)

Note that these pages relate to the accounting period, not the basis period. (The details relating to the basis period would be dealt with on supplementary page 4, but are not assessable.)

HM Revenue & Customs

Self-employment (full)
Tax year 6 April 2013 to 5 April 2014

Please read the *Self-employment (full) notes* to check if you should use this page or the *Self-employment (short)* page.

To get notes and helpsheets that will help you fill in this form, go to hmrc.gov.uk/selfassessmentforms

Your name	Your Unique Taxpayer Reference (UTR)
D e b o r a h B a k e r	

Business details

1 Business name – *unless it is in your own name*

2 Description of business

T r a d e r

3 First line of your business address – *unless you work from home*

4 Postcode of your business address

5 If the details in boxes 1, 2, 3 or 4 have changed in the last 12 months, put 'X' in the box and give details in the 'Any other information' box

6 If your business started after 5 April 2013, enter the start date *DD MM YYYY*

0 1 1 0 2 0 1 4

7 If your business ceased after 5 April 2013 but before 6 April 2014, enter the final date of trading

8 Date your books or accounts start – *the beginning of your accounting period*

0 1 1 0 2 0 1 4

9 Date your books or accounts are made up to or the end of your accounting period – *read the notes if you have filled in box 6 or 7*

3 0 0 9 2 0 1 5

10 If you used the *cash basis*, money actually received and paid out, to calculate your income and expenses put 'X' in the box – *read the notes*

Other information

11 If your accounting date has changed permanently, put 'X' in the box

12 If your accounting date has changed more than once since 2008, put 'X' in the box

13 If special arrangements apply, put 'X' in the box – *read the notes*

14 If you provided the information about your 2013–14 profit on last year's tax return, put 'X' in the box – *read the notes*

Business income

15 Your turnover – *the takings, fees, sales or money earned by your business*

£ 1 9 6 0 0 0 . 0 0

16 Any other business income not included in box 15

£ . 0 0

SA103F 2014   Page SEF 1   HMRC 12/13

Business expenses

Please read the *Self-employment (full) notes* before filling in this section.

Total expenses

If your annual turnover was below £79,000 you may just put your total expenses in box 31

Disallowable expenses

Use this column if the figures in boxes 17 to 30 include disallowable amounts

17 Cost of goods bought for resale or goods used

£ 58 500 · 0 0

32

£ · 0 0

18 Construction industry – *payments to subcontractors*

£ · 0 0

33

£ · 0 0

19 Wages, salaries and other staff costs

£ 43 800 · 0 0

34

£ · 0 0

20 Car, van and travel expenses

£ · 0 0

35

£ · 0 0

21 Rent, rates, power and insurance costs

£ 9 860 · 0 0

36

£ · 0 0

22 Repairs and renewals of property and equipment

£ · 0 0

37

£ · 0 0

23 Phone, fax, stationery and other office costs

£ 2 100 · 0 0

38

£ · 0 0

24 Advertising and business entertainment costs

£ 3 040 · 0 0

39

£ · 0 0

25 Interest on bank and other loans

£ · 0 0

40

£ · 0 0

26 Bank, credit card and other financial charges

£ 1 500 · 0 0

41

£ · 0 0

27 Irrecoverable debts written off

£ · 0 0

42

£ · 0 0

28 Accountancy, legal and other professional fees

£ 2 000 · 0 0

43

£ · 0 0

29 Depreciation and loss/profit on sale of assets

£ 2 900 · 0 0

44

£ · 0 0

30 Other business expenses

£ · 0 0

45

£ · 0 0

31 Total expenses (total of boxes 17 to 30)

£ 123 700 · 0 0

46 Total disallowable expenses (total of boxes 32 to 45)

£ · 0 0

Net profit or loss

47	**Net profit** – *if your business income is more than your expenses (if box 15 + box 16 minus box 31 is positive)*	48	**Or, net loss** – *if your expenses are more than your business income (if box 31 minus (box 15 + box 16) is positive)*
	£ 7 2 3 0 0 · 0 0		£ · 0 0

Tax allowances for vehicles and equipment (capital allowances)

There are 'capital' tax allowances for vehicles, equipment and certain buildings used in your business (don't include the cost of these in your business expenses). Please read the *Self-employment (full) notes* and use the examples to work out your capital allowances.

49	**Annual Investment Allowance**	55	**100% and other enhanced capital allowances** – *read the notes*
	£ · 0 0		£ · 0 0
50	**Capital allowances at 18% on equipment, including cars with lower CO₂ emissions**	56	**Allowances on sale or cessation of business use (where you have disposed of assets for less than their tax value)**
	£ · 0 0		£ · 0 0
51	**Capital allowances at 8% on equipment, including cars with higher CO₂ emissions**	57	**Total capital allowances (total of boxes 49 to 56)**
	£ · 0 0		£ · 0 0
52	**Restricted capital allowances for cars costing more than £12,000** – *if bought before 6 April 2009*	58	**Balancing charge on sale or cessation of business use (only where Business Premises Renovation Allowance has been claimed)** – *read the notes*
	£ · 0 0		£ · 0 0
53	**Agricultural or Industrial Buildings Allowance**	59	**Balancing charge on sales of other assets or on the cessation of business use (where you have disposed of assets for more than their tax value)**
	£ · 0 0		£ · 0 0
54	**Business Premises Renovation Allowance (Assisted Areas only)** – *read the notes*		
	£ · 0 0		

Where I have the subscripts: CO_2 emissions.

Calculating your taxable profit or loss

You may have to adjust your net profit or loss for disallowable expenses or capital allowances to arrive at your taxable profit or your loss for tax purposes. Please read the *Self-employment (full) notes* and fill in the boxes below that apply.

60	**Goods and services for your own use** – *read the notes*	63	**Total deductions from net profit or additions to net loss (box 57 + box 62)**
	£ · 0 0		£ · 0 0
61	**Total additions to net profit or deductions from net loss (box 46 + box 58 + box 59 + box 60)**	64	**Net business profit for tax purposes (if box 47 + box 61 minus (box 48 + box 63) is positive)**
	£ · 0 0		£ · 0 0
62	**Income, receipts and other profits included in business income or expenses but not taxable as business profits**	65	**Net business loss for tax purposes (if box 48 + box 63 minus (box 47 + box 61) is positive)**
	£ · 0 0		£ · 0 0

8   Capital gains tax for individuals

8.1   Select the appropriate procedure for a capital gains tax computation of an individual by ticking the appropriate column. Assume that there is no claim for gift relief where appropriate.

✔

	Use Actual Proceeds	Use market value for proceeds	No gain or loss basis
Sale of asset for £5,000 to a friend. Market value of asset is £20,000			
Gift of asset to friend. Market value of asset is £20,000			
Sale of asset to business partner's wife for £5,000. Market value of asset is £20,000			
Gift of asset to civil partner. Market value of asset is £20,000			
Sale of asset to business partner's grandson for £5,000. Market value of asset is £20,000			
Sale of business asset to an unconnected limited company			
Sale of asset to husband for £20,000. Market value of asset is £5,000			

8.2   Adam purchased and sold shares in Beeco Limited as follows:

- 15 April 2005   Purchased 5,600 shares for £14,560
- 12 January 2015   Sold 1,400 shares for £4,060
- 1 February 2015   Purchased 2,800 shares for £6,160
- 31 March 2015   Sold 7,000 shares for £20,000

(a)   The gain or loss on the sale of shares on 12 January 2015 is

£ [   ]   gain / loss.

(b)   The gain or loss on the sale of shares on 31 March 2015 is

£ [   ]   gain / loss

8.3   Poppy Price is a sole trader. She purchased a warehouse in October 2002 for £280,000, and sold it in April 2014 for £430,000. She purchased a shop in October 2014 for £390,000.

(a)   Complete the following table relating to the gain on the sale of the warehouse, and any deferral of that gain. This was her only capital gain in 2014/15.

	£
Sale proceeds	
Cost	
Total gain	
Deferred gain	
Gain chargeable immediately	
Annual exempt amount	
Amount subject to CGT	

(b)   The cost of the shop will be deemed to be £ ☐ when it is ultimately sold.

8.4   The following statements relate to entrepreneurs' relief. State whether the statements are true or false.

✔

	True	False
(a) It is subject to a lifetime limit of £10,000,000 per individual		
(b) It works by charging the gain at 8%		
(c) All disposals made by an individual are eligible		
(d) It can relate to the disposal of shares held in a 'personal trading company'		
(e) It is subject to a lifetime limit of £100,000,000		
(f) It works by charging the gain at 10%		
(g) It effectively uses up the basic rate band so other gains that are not eligible are more likely to be taxed at 28%		

8.5 There are similarities and differences between chargeable gains for companies subject to Corporation Tax, and Capital Gains Tax for individuals.

Select the rules and reliefs that apply to either or both companies and individuals by ticking the appropriate columns in the following table.

✔

	Companies (Corporation Tax)	Individuals (Capital Gains Tax)
Gift relief		
Rollover relief		
Annual exempt amount		
Indexation allowance		
Chattel rules		
Entrepreneurs' relief		
Part disposal rules		

Chapter activities
answers

1 Introduction to business taxation

1.1 (a), (c) and (e) are correct.

1.2

	Period return relates to	**Latest return submission date**	**Latest tax payment date**
Corporation Tax	Chargeable accounting period	12 months after end of period that accounts are based on	9 months and one day after end of chargeable accounting period
Income Tax	Tax year	31 January following tax year	31 January following tax year

1.3 **(1)** £33,909

(2) £3,114.51

1.4 (a), (b), (c) and (d) are true; (e) and (f) are false.

1.5 The final submission dates for tax returns are as follows:

A sole trader with accounts made up to 31 March 2015: **31 January 2016**

A sole trader with accounts made up to 30 June 2015: **31 January 2017**

A limited company with accounts made up to 31 December 2014: **31 December 2015**

2   Corporation tax – trading profits

2.1

	Add to net profit	Deduct from net profit	No adjustment required
Depreciation	✔		
Discount received			✔
Directors' salaries			✔
Dividends received		✔	
Rent receivable		✔	
Rent payable			✔
Interest payable			✔
Advertising costs			✔
Entertaining customers	✔		

2.2 The adjusted trading profit (before capital allowances) is

(c)   £40,000   *(£37,000 – £12,000 + £13,000 + £2,000)*

2.3 (a), (d) and (g) are true; (b), (c), (e) and (f) are false.

2.4 (e)   shows the correct approach.

2.5 The maximum amount of loss that could be set against the taxable total profits tax for 2013 is

(a) £56,000 *(the loss must first be set against the £25,000 investment income and gains of 2014 before it can be carried back to the previous year)*

3 Corporation tax – capital allowances

3.1

	Qualifying	Not qualifying
Car for employee's private use	✔	
Office furniture	✔	
Capital expenditure on software	✔	
Payments for vehicle on operating lease		✔
Vehicles bought on credit	✔	
Buildings		✔
Equipment bought through hire purchase	✔	

3.2   The AIA that can be claimed is **£60,000**

The first year allowance that can be claimed at 100% is **£26,000**

The writing down allowance that can be claimed at 18% is **£NIL**

The writing down allowance that can be claimed at 8% is **£1,760**

The total capital allowance that can be claimed is **£87,760**

3.3

	AIA (to limit)	Main Pool	Special Rate Pool	100% FYA
Car emissions of 185 g/km			✔	
Car emissions of 99 g/km		✔		
Machinery	✔			
Zero-emission goods vehicle				✔
Car emissions of 125 g/km		✔		
Water-efficient plant				✔

3.4   (b) and (d) are true; (a), (c) and (e) are false.

3.5   **Capital Allowance Computation**

	main pool £	special rate pool £	capital allowances £
WDV bf	120,000	19,000	
add			
Acquisitions			
without FYA or AIA:			
Car (190g/km)		35,000	
Acquisitions			
qualifying for AIA			
Machinery £60,000			
AIA £(60,000)			60,000
Excess -	0		
less			
Proceeds of disposals:	(5,000)	(7,000)	
	115,000	47,000	
18% WDA	(20,700)		20,700
8% WDA		(3,760)	3,760
WDV cf	94,300	43,240	
Total Capital Allowances			84,460

4 Corporation tax – chargeable gains

4.1

	Actual Proceeds	Market Value	£6,000	Zero
Sale of asset for £15,000 to Director who owns 80% of shares in company. Market value of asset is £35,000		✔		
Gift of asset to unconnected individual (non-shareholder)		✔		
Sale of asset to company employee (non-shareholder) at below market value	✔			
Sale of chattel for £4,000 (its market value) that had originally cost £10,000			✔	
Destruction of an uninsured asset during fire				✔
Sale of asset for £15,000 to Director who owns 10% of shares in company. Market value of asset is £35,000	✔			
Shares owned in an unconnected company that have become worthless due to the company's liquidation				✔

4.2   Proceeds: £10,000

Cost: £3,500

Indexation allowance: £1,750

Gain: £4,750

Chattel restriction on gain: £6,667

The chattel restriction will NOT have any effect on the original gain.

4.3

	No. Shares	Cost £	Indexed Cost £
Purchase	8,000	19,500	19,500
Index to July 2003			2,223
Rights issue	200	360	360
Sub total	8,200	19,860	22,083
Index to April 2014			9,054
Sub total	8,200	19,860	31,137
Disposal	(6,000)	(14,532)	(22,783)
Pool balance	2,200	5,328	**8,354**

Proceeds	£24,000
Indexed Cost	£22,783
Gain	£1,217

4.4   Proceeds. £40,000

Cost[1]: £36,000

Indexation allowance: £18,000

Gain or (Loss)[2]: £0

Notes:

(1)   Cost is calculated as £90,000 x £40,000 / (£40,000 + £60,000)

(2)   Indexation cannot create a loss

4.5   Proceeds[1]: £6,000

Cost: £7,500

Indexation allowance[2]: £0

Gain or (Loss): (£1,500)

Notes:

(1)   Deemed proceeds are £6,000 for a chattel sold at a loss for under £6,000

(2)   Indexation allowance cannot be used to increase a loss

5 Corporation tax – calculating the tax

5.1

	£
Corporation Tax at Main Rate	147,000
Marginal Relief	1,750
Corporation Tax Payable	145,250

Marginal Relief working:

$1/400 \times (1,500,000 - 750,000) \times (700,000 / 750,000) = £1,750$

5.2

	£
Maximum of Band	500,000
Corporation Tax at Main Rate	75,600
Marginal Relief	350
Corporation Tax Payable	75,250

Marginal relief working:

$1/400 \times (500,000 - 360,000) \times 1 = £350$

5.3

Loss	Rules that can apply
Trading Loss	(e)
Capital Loss	(f)
Rental Loss	(a)

5.4 See completed form, opposite.

5.5 (b), (c), (e), (f) and (g) are true; (a) and (d) are false.

5.4 Page 2

Company tax calculation

Turnover

1	Total turnover from trade or profession	**1** £	

Income

3	Trading and professional profits	**3** £ 1,350,000	
4	Trading losses brought forward claimed against profits	**4** £ 130,000	
5	Net trading and professional profits		box 3 minus box 4 **5** £1,220,000
6	Bank, building society or other interest, and profits and gains from non-trading loan relationships	**6** £	
11	Income from UK land and buildings	**11** £250,000	
14	Annual profits and gains not falling under any other heading	**14** £	

Chargeable gains

16	Gross chargeable gains	**16** £ 220,000	
17	Allowable losses including losses brought forward	**17** £ 50,000	
18	Net chargeable gains		box 16 minus box 17 **18** £170,000

21	**Profits before other deductions and reliefs**		sum of boxes 5, 6, 11, 14 & 18 **21** £ 1,640,000

Deductions and Reliefs

24	Management expenses under S75 ICTA 1988	**24** £	
30	Trading losses of this or a later accounting period under S393A ICTA 1988	**30** £	
31	Put an 'X' in box 31 if amounts carried back from later accounting periods are included in box 30	**31**	
32	Non-trade capital allowances	**32** £	
35	Charges paid	**35** £	

37	**Profits chargeable to corporation tax**		box 21 minus boxes 24, 30, 32 and 35 **37** £1,640,000

Tax calculation

38	Franked investment income	**38** £200,000	
39	Number of associated companies in this period or	**39** 0	
40	Associated companies in the first financial year	**40**	
41	Associated companies in the second financial year	**41**	
42	Put an 'X' in box 42 if the company claims to be charged at the starting rate or the small companies' rate on any part of its profits, or is claiming marginal rate relief		**42**

Enter how much profit has to be charged and at what rate of tax

Financial year (yyyy)	Amount of profit	Rate of tax	Tax	
43 2 0 1 4	**44** £1,640,000	**45** 21%	**46** £ 344,400	p
53	**54** £	**55**	**56** £	p
			total of boxes 46 and 56 **63** £ 344,400	p

63	Corporation tax		
64	Marginal rate relief	**64** £	p
65	Corporation tax net of marginal rate relief	**65** £ 344,400	p
66	Underlying rate of corporation tax	**66** 21·00 %	
67	Profits matched with non-corporate distributions	**67**	
68	Tax at non-corporate distributions rate	**68** £	p
69	Tax at underlying rate on remaining profits	**69** £	p
70	**Corporation tax chargeable**	See note for box 70 in CT600 Guide **70** £ 344,400	p

CT600 (Short) (2008) Version 2

6 Income tax – trading profits

6.1

	Badges of Trade
Reason for acquisition and sale of item(s)	✔
Whether individual enjoys carrying out the activity	
Whether there is a profit motive	✔
How long the individual has owned the item(s) before sale	✔
Whether the individual only sells via computer sites	
Whether any supplementary work is carried out on the item(s) before sale	✔
Whether the individual considers the activity to be his hobby	
How often the individual carries out similar transactions	✔
Whether the items bought and sold (the subject matter) are used personally by the individual before sale	✔

6.2

	Allowable expenditure	Non-allowable expenditure
Cost of sales	✔	
Entertaining staff	✔	
Fines for lawbreaking by business owner		✔
Gifts of food or drink to customers		✔
Trade bad debts written off	✔	
Salary and NIC of business owner		✔
Depreciation		✔
Loss on sale of non-current assets		✔

6.3

	£	£
Net Profit		112,310
Add		
Goods for own use	2,000	
Depreciation	22,020	
Laura's salary	45,000	
Laura's son's salary (unreasonable)	28,000	
Gifts of bottles of wine	2,400	
Laura's son's car expenses	3,800	
Increase in general bad debt provision	2,600	
		105,820
		218,130
Less		
Capital allowances		10,400
Adjusted trading profits		207,730

6.4 The AIA that can be claimed is **£44,400**[1]

The single asset pool writing down allowance that can be claimed is **£2,160**[2]

The special rate pool writing down allowance that can be claimed is **£0**

The total capital allowance that can be claimed is **£46,560**[3]

The written down value carried forward is **£16,400**[4]

Workings:

(1)   £30,000 + (£18,000 x 80%) = £44,400 (below AIA limit for this period.)

(2)   £20,000 x 18% x 60% = £2,160

(3)   £44,400 + £2,160 = £46,560

(4)   £20,000 – (£20,000 x 18%) = £16,400

6.5 (b)   £37,000

The rules for a sole trader or partnership mean that the loss can be set off against the previous year's total income without first setting off in the current year.

7 Income tax – further issues

7.1 **(a)** The tax year in which he started trading was **2012/13**.

(b) His taxable profits in his first tax year of trading were **£43,000**.

(c) His taxable profits in his second tax year of trading were **£108,000**.

(d) His taxable profits in his third tax year of trading were **£92,000**.

(e) His overlap profits were **£27,000**.

(f) His overlap profits are deducted from the profits in the final year of trading.

7.2 **(d)** 6 April 2013 to 5 April 2014

7.3 **(1)**

	Total	Pete	Heather	Ash
	£	£	£	£
1 Jan – 31 August 2014	80,000	40,000	40,000	0
1 Sept – 31 Dec 2014	40,000	15,000	15,000	10,000
Total	120,000	55,000	55,000	10,000

(2) **(c)** 1/9/2014 - 5/4/2015

7.4

		£
Payment on 31 January 2015	Balance of tax and NIC for 2013/14	3,600
	Payment on account for 2014/15	5,800
	Total	9,400
Payment on 31 July 2015	Payment on account for 2014/15	5,800

7.5

HM Revenue & Customs

Self-employment (full)

Tax year 6 April 2013 to 5 April 2014

Please read the *Self-employment (full) notes* to check if you should use this page or the *Self-employment (short)* page.

To get notes and helpsheets that will help you fill in this form, go to **hmrc.gov.uk/selfassessmentforms**

Your name	Your Unique Taxpayer Reference (UTR)
Deborah Baker	

Business details

1 Business name – *unless it is in your own name*

2 Description of business

Trader

3 First line of your business address – *unless you work from home*

4 Postcode of your business address

5 If the details in boxes 1, 2, 3 or 4 have changed in the last 12 months, put 'X' in the box and give details in the 'Any other information' box

6 If your business started after 5 April 2013, enter the start date *DD MM YYYY*

01 10 2014

7 If your business ceased after 5 April 2013 but before 6 April 2014, enter the final date of trading

8 Date your books or accounts start – *the beginning of your accounting period*

01 10 2014

9 Date your books or accounts are made up to or the end of your accounting period – *read the notes if you have filled in box 6 or 7*

30 09 2015

10 If you used the *cash basis*, money actually received and paid out, to calculate your Income and expenses put 'X' in the box – *read the notes*

Other information

11 If your accounting date has changed permanently, put 'X' in the box

12 If your accounting date has changed more than once since 2008, put 'X' in the box

13 If special arrangements apply, put 'X' in the box – *read the notes*

14 If you provided the information about your 2013-14 profit on last year's tax return, put 'X' in the box – *read the notes*

Business income

15 Your turnover – *the takings, fees, sales or money earned by your business*

£ 196000.00

16 Any other business income not included in box 15

£ .00

Business expenses

Please read the *Self-employment (full) notes* before filling in this section.

	Total expenses		Disallowable expenses
	If your annual turnover was below £79,000 you may just put your total expenses in box 31		Use this column if the figures in boxes 17 to 30 include disallowable amounts

	Total expenses		Disallowable expenses
17 Cost of goods bought for resale or goods used	£ 58 500 . 0 0	**32**	£ . 0 0
18 Construction industry – *payments to subcontractors*	£ . 0 0	**33**	£ . 0 0
19 Wages, salaries and other staff costs	£ 43 800 . 0 0	**34**	£ 20 000 . 0 0
20 Car, van and travel expenses	£ . 0 0	**35**	£ . 0 0
21 Rent, rates, power and insurance costs	£ 9 860 . 0 0	**36**	£ . 0 0
22 Repairs and renewals of property and equipment	£ . 0 0	**37**	£ . 0 0
23 Phone, fax, stationery and other office costs	£ 2 100 . 0 0	**38**	£ 400 . 0 0
24 Advertising and business entertainment costs	£ 3 040 . 0 0	**39**	£ 1 600 . 0 0
25 Interest on bank and other loans	£ . 0 0	**40**	£ . 0 0
26 Bank, credit card and other financial charges	£ 1 500 . 0 0	**41**	£ 530 . 0 0
27 Irrecoverable debts written off	£ . 0 0	**42**	£ . 0 0
28 Accountancy, legal and other professional fees	£ 2 000 . 0 0	**43**	£ . 0 0
29 Depreciation and loss/profit on sale of assets	£ 2 900 . 0 0	**44**	£ 2 900 . 0 0
30 Other business expenses	£ . 0 0	**45**	£ . 0 0
31 Total expenses (total of boxes 17 to 30)	£ 123 700 . 0 0	**46** Total disallowable expenses (total of boxes 32 to 45)	£ 25 430 . 0 0

Net profit or loss

47 Net profit – *if your business income is more than your expenses (if box 15 + box 16 minus box 31 is positive)*

£ 7 2 3 0 0 · 0 0

48 Or, net loss – *if your expenses are more than your business income (if box 31 minus (box 15 + box 16) is positive)*

£ · 0 0

Tax allowances for vehicles and equipment (capital allowances)

There are 'capital' tax allowances for vehicles, equipment and certain buildings used in your business (don't include the cost of these in your business expenses). Please read the *Self-employment (full) notes* and use the examples to work out your capital allowances.

49 Annual Investment Allowance

£ 2 9 0 0 0 · 0 0

50 Capital allowances at 18% on equipment, including cars with lower CO_2 emissions

£ · 0 0

51 Capital allowances at 8% on equipment, including cars with higher CO_2 emissions

£ · 0 0

52 Restricted capital allowances for cars costing more than £12,000 – *if bought before 6 April 2009*

£ · 0 0

53 Agricultural or Industrial Buildings Allowance

£ · 0 0

54 Business Premises Renovation Allowance (Assisted Areas only) – *read the notes*

£ · 0 0

55 100% and other enhanced capital allowances – *read the notes*

£ · 0 0

56 Allowances on sale or cessation of business use (where you have disposed of assets for less than their tax value)

£ · 0 0

57 Total capital allowances (total of boxes 49 to 56)

£ 2 9 0 0 0 · 0 0

58 Balancing charge on sale or cessation of business use (only where Business Premises Renovation Allowance has been claimed) – *read the notes*

£ · 0 0

59 Balancing charge on sales of other assets or on the cessation of business use (where you have disposed of assets for more than their tax value)

£ · 0 0

Calculating your taxable profit or loss

You may have to adjust your net profit or loss for disallowable expenses or capital allowances to arrive at your taxable profit or your loss for tax purposes. Please read the *Self-employment (full) notes* and fill in the boxes below that apply.

60 Goods and services for your own use – *read the notes*

£ · 0 0

61 Total additions to net profit or deductions from net loss (box 46 + box 58 + box 59 + box 60)

£ 2 5 4 3 0 · 0 0

62 Income, receipts and other profits included in business income or expenses but not taxable as business profits

£ · 0 0

63 Total deductions from net profit or additions to net loss (box 57 + box 62)

£ 2 9 0 0 0 · 0 0

64 Net business profit for tax purposes (if box 47 + box 61 minus (box 48 + box 63) is positive)

£ 6 8 7 3 0 · 0 0

65 Net business loss for tax purposes (if box 48 + box 63 minus (box 47 + box 61) is positive)

£ · 0 0

8 Capital gains tax for individuals

8.1

	Use Actual Proceeds	Use market value for proceeds	No gain or loss basis
Sale of asset for £5,000 to a friend. Market value of asset is £20,000	✔		
Gift of asset to friend. Market value of asset is £20,000		✔	
Sale of asset to business partner's wife for £5,000. Market value of asset is £20,000		✔	
Gift of asset to civil partner. Market value of asset is £20,000			✔
Sale of asset to business partner's grandson for £5,000. Market value of asset is £20,000		✔	
Sale of business asset to an unconnected limited company	✔		
Sale of asset to husband for £20,000. Market value of asset is £5,000			✔

8.2 **(a)** The **gain** on the sale of shares on 12 January 2015 is **£980**.

The shares sold on 12 January are matched with 1,400 of those bought on 1 February (within the following 30 days), leaving 1,400 of that purchase unmatched.

(b) The **gain** on the sale of shares on 31 March 2015 is **£2,360**.

The shares sold on 31 March are matched with the pooled purchases of 5,600 + 1,400 (balance) = 7,000 shares, costing a total of £17,640.

8.3 **(a)**

	£
Sale proceeds	430,000
Cost	280,000
Total gain	150,000
Deferred gain	110,000
Gain chargeable immediately	40,000
Annual exempt amount	11,000
Amount subject to CGT	29,000

(b) The cost of the shop will be deemed to be £280,000 when it is ultimately sold.
(£390,000 - £110,000).

8.4 (a), (d), (f) and (g) are true; (b), (c) and (e) are false.

8.5

	Companies (Corporation Tax)	Individuals (Capital Gains Tax)
Gift relief		✔
Rollover relief	✔	✔
Annual exempt amount		✔
Indexation allowance	✔	
Chattel rules	✔	✔
Entrepreneurs' relief		✔
Part disposal rules	✔	✔

Practice
assessment 1

Task 1

Lesley Lampeter is a sole trader. Her business has the following statement of profit or loss:

	£	£
Turnover		1,150,000
Cost of sales		758,450
Gross profit		391,550
Wages and salaries	112,510	
Rent, rates and insurance	40,350	
Advertising and entertaining	11,585	
Professional fees	5,060	
Motor expenses	50,030	
Telephone and office costs	33,050	
Depreciation	22,680	
Other expenses	30,310	305,575
Net Profit		85,975

Notes:

1. Lesley took goods from the business that cost £1,000 and would normally sell for £1,750. The cost has already been excluded from cost of sales.

2. Wages and salaries include: £
    Lesley's class 2 NIC contributions 140
    Lesley's pension contributions 7,985

3. Advertising and entertaining includes: £
    Gifts to customers:
        Bottles of whisky costing £28 each 2,800
        400 calendars carrying the business's logo 1,200

4. Professional fees include: £
    Costs incurred in tax appeal 2,500

5. Motor expenses include: £
    Lesley's car expenses (used 50% for business) 3,900

6. Other expenses include: £
    Bad debts written off 1,450
    Increase in specific bad debt provision 2,000

7. Capital allowances have already been calculated at £20,680

Complete the adjusted trading profits computation.

Task 2

A company has the following information regarding its non-current assets for a 12-month CAP, ending on 30/6/2014.

	£
Written down values brought forward:	
General (main) pool	105,000
Special rate pool	17,000
Additions:	
Computer System (bought January 2014)	290,000
New car for Sales Director (emissions 89 g/km)	25,000
Disposals:	
Machinery	5,000

Calculate the maximum capital allowances for the CAP.

Task 3(a)

Cherie started trading on 1 October 2012. She makes up her accounts to 31 December. The profits were calculated as:

	£
Period to 31 December 2013	120,000
Year to 31 December 2014	84,000
Year to 31 December 2015	99,000

(1) The tax year in which she started trading was *(select one)*:

2010/11; 2011/12; 2012/13; 2013/14

(2) Her taxable profits in her first tax year of trading were *(select one)*:

£24,000; £48,000; £96,000; £120,000

(3) Her taxable profits in her second tax year of trading were *(select one)*:

£84,000; £96,000; £99,000; £120,000

(4) Her taxable profits in her third tax year of trading were *(select one)*:

£84,000; £87,750; £93,000; £99,000

(5) Her overlap profits were   £ ⬜

(b)

Ivor, Jo and Kirsty have been in partnership for many years, sharing profits in the ratio 5:3:2. They have always made their accounts up to 31 December each year.

On 31 July 2014, Kirsty decided to leave the partnership. The remaining partners then agreed to divide their profits equally.

For the year ended 31 December 2013, the partnership trading profit was £96,000.

For the year ended 31 December 2014, the partnership trading profit was £120,000.

Kirsty had no overlap profits brought forward.

(1) Using the following table, calculate the division of profits between the partners for the accounting year ended 31 December 2014.

	Total £	Ivor £	Jo £	Kirsty £
1 Jan – 31 July 2014				
1 Aug – 31 Dec 2014				
Total				

(2) What is the trading assessment for 2014/15 for Kirsty?

£

Task 4(a)

Delta Limited has produced the following results for the 16-month accounting period to 31 December 2014.

Trading Profits for 16-month period		
(before capital allowances)		£800,000
Capital Allowances:	y/e 31/8/2014	£54,000
	4 months to 31/12/2014	£19,000
Chargeable Gains:	Disposal 12/12/2013	£36,000
	Disposal 19/4/2014	£14,000
	Disposal 10/10/2014	£41,000
Rental Income – monthly amount		£2,000
Gift Aid Payment (paid 31/12/2014)		£6,000

Use the following table to calculate the TTP for each CAP.

	CAP 12 months to 31/8/2014 £	CAP 4 months to 31/12/2014 £
Trading Profits before CAs		
Capital Allowances		
Trading Profits		
Chargeable Gains		
Rental Income		
Sub total		
Gift Aid		
TTP		

(b)

Gamma Ltd is a trading company with two associated companies. It has the following results for the 6 month CAP to 31/12/2014.

	£
Trading Profits	130,000
Chargeable Gains	25,000
Gift Aid Payments	15,000

Calculate the corporation tax using the following table.

	£
Maximum of Band	
Minimum of Band	
Corporation Tax at Main Rate	
Marginal Relief	
Corporation Tax Payable	

Task 5

Which of the following statements are correct?

		✔
(a)	Every self employed taxpayer must pay Class 2 NIC, unless the profits are more than £41,865	
(b)	Class 4 NIC is payable by the self employed at 9% on profits between £7,956 and £41,865	
(c)	Class 4 NIC is payable at 2% on any drawings over £41,865	
(d)	Class 4 NIC is subject to the same system of payment as income tax for sole traders	
(e)	Class 4 NIC is payable at 2% on profits over £41,865	
(f)	Class 2 NIC may be paid monthly by direct debit	

Task 6

A sole trader has the following tax-adjusted results for the tax years 2013/14 and 2014/15:

	2013/14	2014/15
Trading Profits	£12,000	£0
Other Income	£19,000	£21,000

The sole trader incurred a trading loss in 2014/15 of £38,000.

Which one of the following statements shows the full options for the amount of the loss that could be set against the individual's income for 2013/14?

		✔
(a)	any amount up to £31,000	
(b)	any amount up to £17,000	
(c)	any amount up to £19,000	
(d)	either £12,000 or nothing	
(e)	either £31,000 or £17,000 or nothing	
(f)	either £17,000 or nothing	
(g)	either £17,000 or £12,000 or nothing	
(h)	£0 only	

Task 7

It is May 2015. A new client, David, has come to you to ask advice. David is a Director of a limited company that started trading on 1 January 2013. HMRC were notified that trading had started, but no other contact has been made with HMRC regarding Corporation Tax.

Accounts have been prepared for the year ended 31 December 2013 and it has been calculated that the Corporation Tax for that period will be £45,000. Unfortunately, since the accounts were prepared many of the sales and purchase invoices for the period were accidentally shredded.

Write a note that explains what deadlines have been missed and what penalties and / or interest the company could be liable for based on the above information.

Task 8

Alison Amsterdam and Bob Bolton have been trading in partnership for many years with accounting year ends of 31 March. They trade in wholesale fabric. The trade profits and taxed interest received are both divided between the partners in the ratio 3:2.

In the accounting year ended 31/3/2015, the partnership had trade profits of £80,000 and received taxed interest of £2,000 gross (£1,600 net).

Complete page 6 of the partnership tax return (the 2013/14 version is reproduced on the opposite page) relating to:

- the whole partnership, and

- Alison Amsterdam's share of profits and income.

PARTNERSHIP STATEMENT (SHORT) *for the year ended 5 April 2014*

Please read these instructions before completing the Statement

Use these pages to allocate partnership income if the only income for the relevant return period was trading and professional income or taxed interest and alternative finance receipts from banks and building societies. Otherwise you must download or ask the SA Orderline for the *Partnership Statement (Full)* pages to record details of the allocation of all the partnership income. Go to **hmrc.gov.uk/selfassessmentforms**

Step 1   Fill in boxes 1 to 29 and boxes A and B as appropriate. Get the figures you need from the relevant boxes in the Partnership Tax Return. Complete a separate Statement for each accounting period covered by this Partnership Tax Return and for each trade or profession carried on by the partnership.

Step 2   Then allocate the amounts in boxes 11 to 29 attributable to each partner using the allocation columns on this page and page 7, read the Partnership Tax Return Guide, go to **hmrc.gov.uk/selfassessmentforms** If the partnership has more than three partners, please photocopy page 7.

Step 3   Each partner will need a copy of their allocation of income to fill in their personal tax return.

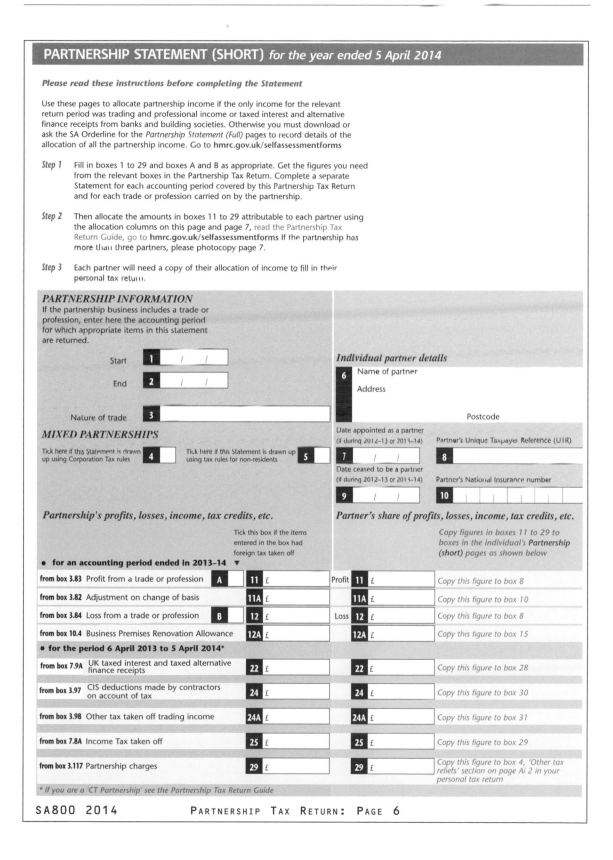

PARTNERSHIP INFORMATION

If the partnership business includes a trade or profession, enter here the accounting period for which appropriate items in this statement are returned.

Start **1** / /

End **2** / /

Nature of trade **3**

MIXED PARTNERSHIPS

Tick here if this Statement is drawn up using Corporation Tax rules **4**

Tick here if this Statement is drawn up using tax rules for non-residents **5**

Individual partner details

6 Name of partner

Address

Postcode

Date appointed as a partner
(if during 2012–13 or 2013–14)

7 / /

Partner's Unique Taxpayer Reference (UTR)

8

Date ceased to be a partner
(if during 2012–13 or 2013–14)

9 / /

Partner's National Insurance number

10

Partnership's profits, losses, income, tax credits, etc.

Tick this box if the items entered in the box had foreign tax taken off

Partner's share of profits, losses, income, tax credits, etc.

Copy figures in boxes 11 to 29 to boxes in the individual's Partnership (short) pages as shown below

- **for an accounting period ended in 2013–14** ▼

from box 3.83 Profit from a trade or profession **A**	**11** £	Profit **11** £	*Copy this figure to box 8*
from box 3.82 Adjustment on change of basis	**11A** £	**11A** £	*Copy this figure to box 10*
from box 3.84 Loss from a trade or profession **B**	**12** £	Loss **12** £	*Copy this figure to box 8*
from box 10.4 Business Premises Renovation Allowance	**12A** £	**12A** £	*Copy this figure to box 15*

- **for the period 6 April 2013 to 5 April 2014***

from box 7.9A UK taxed interest and taxed alternative finance receipts	**22** £	**22** £	*Copy this figure to box 28*
from box 3.97 CIS deductions made by contractors on account of tax	**24** £	**24** £	*Copy this figure to box 30*
from box 3.98 Other tax taken off trading income	**24A** £	**24A** £	*Copy this figure to box 31*
from box 7.8A Income Tax taken off	**25** £	**25** £	*Copy this figure to box 29*
from box 3.117 Partnership charges	**29** £	**29** £	*Copy this figure to box 4, 'Other tax reliefs' section on page Ai 2 in your personal tax return*

* *If you are a 'CT Partnership' see the Partnership Tax Return Guide*

Task 9(a)

Analyse the following assets into those that are chargeable regarding CGT and those that are exempt.

✔

	Chargeable	Exempt
Government Stocks (gilts)		
Shares in Limited Companies		
Trading Inventory		
Land		

(b)

Trolley Ltd sold an antique painting for £7,100 in April 2014. This was bought for £4,000 in August 2000. The indexation factor from August 2000 to April 2014 was 0.500.

Complete the following computation:

Proceeds   £

Cost   £

Indexation allowance   £

Gain   £

Chattel restriction on gain   £

State whether the chattel restriction will have any effect on the original gain.   YES / NO

Task 10(a)

Perfect Ltd bought 9,000 shares in Toronto Ltd for £27,900 in October 2001. Bonus shares were issued in April 2002 at 1 for 10. Purchases of 5,000 shares were made in July 2003 for £3.80 per share. In April 2014, Perfect Ltd sold 10,000 of the shares for £5.00 per share.

Indexation factors were:

October 2001 to July 2003:	0.114
July 2003 to April 2014:	0.410

Calculate the pool balances remaining and the gain made on the share disposal.

	No. Shares	Cost £	Indexed Cost £

Proceeds	£
Indexed Cost	£
Gain	£

Task 10(b)

Carol purchased and sold shares in Ceeco Limited as follows:

10 April 2002	Purchased 5,000 shares for £15,000
12 January 2015	Sold 1,800 shares for £4,000
1 February 2015	Purchased 6,800 shares for £21,080
31 March 2015	Sold 10,000 shares for £40,000

(1) The gain or loss on the sale of shares on 12 January 2015 is

£ [   ] gain / loss.

(2) The gain or loss on the sale of shares on 31 March 2015 is

£ [   ] gain / loss

Task 11

Polly Prince is a sole trader. She purchased a warehouse in October 2000 for £180,000, and sold it in September 2014 for £400,000. She had purchased a shop in October 2013 for £335,000. The disposal of the warehouse is eligible for entrepreneurs' relief. Polly has not previously made any claims for entrepreneurs' relief.

(a)   Complete the following table relating to the gain on the sale of the warehouse, and deferral of that gain (if any). This was her only capital gain in 2014/15.

	£
Sale proceeds	
Cost	
Total gain	
Deferred gain	
Gain chargeable immediately	
Annual exempt amount	
Capital Gains Tax payable	

(b)   The cost of the shop will be deemed to be £ ☐ when it is ultimately sold.

Practice
assessment 2

Task 1

Lisa has the following income statement:

	£	£
Gross profit		1,450,395
Wages and salaries	731,200	
Accountancy and legal costs	21,450	
Motor expenses	65,480	
Repairs and renewals	55,550	
Office expenses	42,690	
Depreciation	155,310	
Other expenses	41,840	1,113,520
Profit		336,875

Notes include:

Gross profit is after deducting bulk discounts given of　　　　　£15,300

Wages and salaries include:
Lisa's salary and personal pension contributions　　　　　£75,400
Lisa's son's salary (he works part time in the office)　　　　　£7,400

Accountancy and legal costs comprise:
Legal fees to purchase new office building　　　　　£10,250
Annual accountancy and audit fee　　　　　£11,200

Motor expenses include:
Operating lease of 180g/km car used for business by works manager　　£11,660
Expenses of Lisa's car which is used 70% for the business　　　　£12,500

Repairs and renewals include:
Repainting exterior of factory building　　　　　£40,000

Capital allowances have been calculated as　　　　　£21,380

(a)

Complete the following computation. You may not need to use all the lines provided.

	£
Profit	336,875
Disallowed items added back:	
Allowed items deducted:	
Adjusted trading profits	

(b)

Complete the following table by selecting the correct treatment of each item in the accounts of a sole trader when adjusting for tax purposes.

✔

	Add back to profit	Deduct from profit	No adjustment required
Loss on sale of non-current assets			
Installation costs of new machinery			
Discounts received for prompt payment			
Interest received on deposit account			

Task 2

Tintagel Limited had the following non-current asset information for the seven month period ending on 31 December 2014.

Balances brought forward on 1 June 2014:

General pool	£157,500
Special rate pool	£31,680

Additions during period:

Machinery	£314,334
Car (CO_2 emissions 89g/km)	£29,500

The company was forced to cease trading on 30 April 2015, following an irrecoverable debt from a major customer.

The proceeds of the non-current assets that were sold on that date were:

Car purchased in previous CAP	£19,800
General pool machinery	£55,500
Special rate pool items	£22,100

Calculate the capital allowances for the CAP ended 31 December 2014, and the final CAP ended 30 April 2015.

Task 3

Gina commenced trading on 1 February 2013. Her taxable profits have been agreed for her accounting periods as follows:

Period to 31 October 2013	£88,200
Year ended 31 October 2014	£133,200
Year ended 31 October 2015	£107,400

Calculate the basis periods and the assessable profits for each of the first three tax years of Gina's business, and complete the following table:

	Tax year	Basis period							Profit
	YYYY/YY	Day	Month	YYYY		Day	Month	YYYY	£
1st year	2012/13	01	February	2013	-	05	April	2013	19,600
2nd year	2013/14	01	February	2013	-	31	January	2014	121,500
3rd year	2014/15	01	November	2013	-	31	October	2014	133,200

The overlap profit is   £ 52,900

Task 4(a)

Team Limited made up accounts for the 17 month period to 28 February 2015. The following details have been extracted for the period:

The company made a capital loss of £14,150 in September 2014, and capital gains of £19,660 in July 2014 and £19,475 in December 2014. The adjusted trading profits for the period were £160,871.

State the amounts to be taken into account in each of the following periods.

	First accounting period £	Second accounting period £
Capital gains		
Trading profits		

(b)

Indicate whether the following statement is true or false:

Dividends received from associated companies are ignored when calculating the augmented profits for a company.

TRUE / FALSE

(c)

A company has the following information for the 9 month period ended 31 March 2015:

- Taxable total profits £345,500
- Dividends received from non-associated companies £27,900
- Dividends received from associated company £36,000
- The company has one associated company

Complete the following tables to calculate the Corporation Tax payable:

Data	£
Augmented profits	
Maximum of relevant band	

	£
Corporation tax at main rate	
Marginal relief	
Corporation tax payable	

Task 5

The partnership agreement of Brian and Colin stipulates that Brian is entitled to 55% of partnership profits and Colin 45%.

The total partnership profits for 2014/15 were £89,600.

Complete the following table and calculate the Class 4 National Insurance Contributions for both Brian and Colin for 2014/15. Calculations should be carried out to the nearest penny.

	Profits £	Class 4 at 9% £	Class 4 at 2% £	Total Class 4 NIC £
Brian				
Colin				

Task 6

Tulip Limited has the following results from the last two years.

Year ended	31 March 2015 £	31 March 2014 £
Trading profit (loss)	(41,250)	10,680
Chargeable gain (loss)	(5,650)	15,400
Rental profit	12,000	12,000
Gift aid	1,800	1,800

Tulip Limited has a policy of always claiming relief for losses as soon as possible.

Complete the following table to show how Tulip Limited would claim for their losses.

	£
How much trading loss can be claimed against income in the year ended 31 March 2015?	
How much trading loss can be claimed against income in the year ended 31 March 2014?	
How much trading loss can be carried forward to the year ended 31 March 2016?	
How much capital loss can be carried forward against capital gains in the year ended 31 March 2016?	
How much gift aid can be set against income in the year ended 31 March 2014?	
How much gift aid can be set against income in the year ended 31 March 2015?	
How much gift aid can be carried forward to be set against income in the year ended 31 March 2016?	

Task 7

You work for Craister Limited, a company that has had taxable total profits of over £3 million in each of the last 5 years. Craister Limited does not have any associated companies. A new employee has joined the Accountancy Section who has no knowledge of the relevant Corporation Tax payment rules for companies like Craister Limited.

The company has the following final and estimated Corporation Tax liabilities for the current and previous CAPs:

Year ended 31 January 2016   Estimated Corporation Tax   £720,000

Year ended 31 January 2015   Final Corporation Tax   £935,000

The Corporation tax for the year ended 31 January 2015 was originally estimated at £920,000.

It is now June 2015. Explain to the new employee how Corporation Tax dates and amounts of payment are calculated. Also explain what the future payments based on the above figures will amount to and when they must be paid. You do not need to explain how Corporation Tax estimates are arrived at.

Task 8

Fizz Limited has the following information for the year ended 31 December 2014:

Taxable total profits	£1,635,000
Dividends received	£27,000

Fizz Limited has no associated companies.

Complete the relevant boxes on the following return for Fizz Limited. Ignore any pence.

		box 21 minus boxes 24, 30, 32 and 35
37 Profits chargeable to corporation tax		37 £

Tax calculation

38 Franked investment income	38 £	
39 Number of associated companies in this period or	39	
40 Associated companies in the first financial year	40	
41 Associated companies in the second financial year	41	
42 *Put an 'X' in box 42 if the company claims to be charged at the starting rate or the small companies' rate on any part of its profits, or is claiming marginal rate relief*		42

Enter how much profit has to be charged and at what rate of tax

Financial year *(yyyy)*	Amount of profit	Rate of tax	Tax	
43	44 £	45	46 £	p
53	54 £	55	56 £	p

		total of boxes 46 and 56
63 Corporation tax		63 £ p

Task 9(a)

Dickinson Limited sold an asset in April 2014 for £43,500. The costs of disposal were £300. The asset was bought in August 2000 for £19,850 plus buying costs of £650.

The indexation factor from August 2000 to April 2014 is 0.500.

Calculate the chargeable gain on the disposal of this asset using the following table. Enter zero against any costs that are not allowable.

	£	£
Proceeds		
Disposal costs		
Cost		
Buying costs		
Indexation allowance		
Gain		

(b)

Indicate whether each of the following statements is true or false.

	True	False
Indexation allowance does not apply to individuals under CGT		
A limited company can set an annual exempt amount against its gains		

Task 10

Neil bought 3,000 shares in Crossfield Limited in April 1998 for £3 each. In July 2002 there was a bonus issue of 1 for 3 shares. Neil sold 800 shares in the company in August 2003. In January 2012 Neil bought a further 5,000 shares for a total of £23,200.

In June 2014 Neil sold 2,500 shares in Crossfield Limited for a total of £14,850.

Calculate the chargeable gain on the sale of the shares in June 2014. Show the number and cost of the shares still held at that time in your workings.

Task 11

Two taxpayers each made a capital gain in 2014/15 of £35,000 before deducting their annual exempt amount. The amount of their taxable income (after deducting their personal allowance) is shown in the table below.

Calculate the amount of capital gains tax payable by each individual using the following table.

Taxpayer	Taxable income £	Gains chargeable at 18% £	Gains chargeable at 28% £	Total CGT payable £
Sonia	18,500			
Steve	41,250			

Practice
assessment 3

Task 1(a)

Analyse the tax treatment of the following items in a sole trader's trading income computation by ticking the appropriate column.

	Add back to net profit	Deduct from net profit	No adjustment required
Bank interest receivable			
Bank interest payable			
Increase in general provision for irrecoverable debts			
Profit on sale of non-current assets			
Staff travelling expenses			
Owner's class 2 & 4 NIC			
Discounts receivable			

Task 1(b)

Lemming Limited has the following statement of profit or loss:

	£	£
Gross profit		1,980,560
Wages and salaries	863,200	
Accountancy and legal costs	48,450	
Motor expenses	121,680	
Repairs and renewals	130,500	
Office expenses	82,600	
Depreciation	245,110	
Other expenses	88,840	1,580,380
Profit		400,180

Notes include:

Wages and salaries include:

Directors' salaries and personal pension contributions   £175,000

Accountancy and legal costs include:

Legal fees to renew 10 year lease on office building   £4,120

Taxation advice   £3,550

Annual accountancy and audit fee   £11,200

Motor expenses include:

Operating lease of 180g/km car used for business
by Director (50% private use)   £9,860

Repairs and renewals include:

Replacement of office furniture   £12,000

Capital allowances have been calculated as   £33,780

Complete the following computation. You may not need to use all the lines provided.

	£
Profit	400,180
Disallowed items added back:	
Allowed items deducted:	
Adjusted trading profits	

Task 2

A company has the following information regarding its non-current assets for an 8-month CAP ending on 30/4/2014.

Written down values brought forward:

General (main) pool	125,000
Special rate pool	47,000

Additions:

Computer System (bought April 2014)	325,833
New car for Sales Director (emissions 170 g/km)	28,000

Disposals:

Machinery	5,000

Calculate the total capital allowances and show the balances to carry forward to the next accounting period.

Task 3(a)

Cherie started trading on 1 February 2013. She makes up her accounts to 31 December. The profits were calculated as:

	£
Period to 31 December 2013	93,500
Year to 31 December 2014	84,000
Year to 31 December 2015	60,000

Complete the following table by inserting tax years and taxable profits together with the amount of any overlap profits.

	Tax year	Amount £
First year of trading		
Second year of trading		
Third year of trading		
Overlap profits		

(b)

Adam, Ben and Clive have been in partnership for many years, sharing profits in the ratio 5:3:2. They have always made their accounts up to 31 December each year.

On 31 May 2014, Clive left the partnership. On 1 June 2014 Catherine joined the partnership, and all the partners then agreed to divide their profits equally.

For the year ended 31 December 2014, the partnership trading profit was £360,000.

For the year ended 31 December 2015, the partnership trading profit was £396,000.

Clive had no overlap profits brought forward.

(1)   Using the following table, calculate the division of profits between the partners for the accounting year ended 31 December 2014.

	Total £	Adam £	Ben £	Clive £	Catherine £
Period to 31 May					
Period from 1 June					
Total					

(2)   Insert the assessable profits for each partner for the tax year 2014/15 into the following table.

	Assessable profits £
Adam	
Ben	
Clive	
Catherine	

Task 4(a)

Florinda Limited has produced the following results for the 17-month accounting period to 31 December 2014.

Trading Profits for 17-month period (before capital allowances)		£714,000
Capital Allowances:	y/e 31/7/2014	£74,000
	5 months to 31/12/2014	£41,000
Chargeable Gains:	Disposal 12/12/2013	£33,000
	Disposal 19/6/2014	(£44,000) loss
	Disposal 10/11/2014	£17,000
Rental Income – monthly amount		£3,100
Gift Aid Payment (paid 31/12/2014)		£6,000

Use the following table to calculate the TTP for each CAP.

	CAP 12 months to 31/7/2014 £	CAP 5 months to 31/12/2014 £
Trading Profits before CAs		
Capital Allowances		
Trading Profits		
Chargeable Gains		
Rental Income		
Sub total		
Gift Aid		
TTP		

(b)

Gemma Ltd is a trading company with no associated companies. It has the following results for the 12 month CAP to 31/12/2014.

	£
Trading Profits	1,230,000
Chargeable Gains	45,000
Gift Aid Payments	15,000
Dividends received	180,000

Calculate the corporation tax (to the nearest £) using the following table.

	Financial Year 2013 £	Financial Year 2014 £	Total £
Corporation Tax at Full Rate			
Marginal Relief			
Corporation Tax Payable			

Task 5

Decide whether each of the following statements is true or false and tick the appropriate box.

✔

		True	False
(a)	A 75 year old sole trader will not pay class 2 or class 4 NIC		
(b)	Class 4 NIC is payable at a flat weekly rate		
(c)	Class 4 NIC is based on 2% of profits between £7,956 and £41,865, and 9% of profits above that		
(d)	A sole trader with profits of £7,000 would pay class 2 NIC but not class 4 NIC		

Task 6

A limited company has the following tax-adjusted results for the 12 month CAPs ending on 31 December:

	2013 £	2014 £	2015 £
Trading profits	120,500	0	375,000
Trading loss		85,000	
Chargeable gain	50,300		
Capital loss		20,100	
Rental income	10,800	12,400	14,200

Assuming that the company wishes to claim any loss relief as early as possible, complete the following table. Insert zeros into any cells that do not apply.

	2013 £	2014 £	2015 £
Trading profits			
Trading loss offset against trading profits only			
Net chargeable gains			
Rental income			
Trading loss offset against taxable total profits			
Taxable total profits after offsetting losses			

Task 7

It is November 2015.

Josie is a new client. She has approached you for information about her future tax payments, and is worried about what will happen if she cannot afford to pay these amounts.

Josie has provided you with the following information about the self assessment payments that she has already made:

- Paid 31 January 2015:

  2013/14 Balancing payment £9,800 + First payment on account for 2014/15 £11,900 = Total £21,700.

- Paid 31 July 2015:

  Second payment on account for 2014/15 £11,900

You have completed the draft tax computations for Josie for 2014/15 and calculate that the total income tax payable for the tax year will be £31,630.

Explain the amounts that will be payable on 31 January 2016 and 31 July 2016 and how they are calculated. Also explain briefly the implications of not making these payments when due.

Explanations of the amounts payable

Implications of not making payments when due

Task 8

Bryson Limited has a 12 month CAP ending on 31/3/2015.

It has the following tax adjusted results for that period:

Trading Profits	£1,830,000
Trading Loss brought forward	£130,000
Rental Income	£110,000
Chargeable Gains	£89,000
Capital Loss brought forward	£13,000
Gift Aid payment	£ 40,000

Bryson Limited has no associated companies.

Complete, as far as possible, page 2 of the CT600 form for Bryson Limited, including the calculation of Corporation Tax.

Company tax calculation

Turnover

1   Total turnover from trade or profession   **1** £

Income

3   Trading and professional profits   **3** £

4   Trading losses brought forward claimed against profits   **4** £

| | box 3 minus box 4 |

5   Net trading and professional profits   **5** £

6   Bank, building society or other interest, and profits and
    gains from non-trading loan relationships   **6** £

11 Income from UK land and buildings   **11** £

14 Annual profits and gains not falling under any other heading   **14** £

Chargeable gains

16 Gross chargeable gains   **16** £

17 Allowable losses including losses brought forward   **17** £

| | box 16 minus box 17 |

18 Net chargeable gains   **18** £

| | sum of boxes 5, 6, 11, 14 & 18 |

21 Profits before other deductions and reliefs   **21** £

Deductions and Reliefs

24 Management expenses under S75 ICTA 1988   **24** £

30 Trading losses of this or a later accounting period
    under S393A ICTA 1988   **30** £

31 Put an 'X' in box 31 if amounts carried back from later
    accounting periods are included in box 30   **31**

32 Non-trade capital allowances   **32** £

35 Charges paid   **35** £

| | box 21 minus boxes 24, 30, 32 and 35 |

37 Profits chargeable to corporation tax   **37** £

Tax calculation

38 Franked investment income   **38** £

39 Number of associated companies in this period   **39**
    or

40 Associated companies in the first financial year   **40**

41 Associated companies in the second financial year   **41**

42 Put an 'X' in box 42 if the company claims to be charged at the starting rate or the
    small companies' rate on any part of its profits, or is claiming marginal rate relief   **42**

Enter how much profit has to be charged and at what rate of tax

Financial year (yyyy)	Amount of profit	Rate of tax	Tax	
43	**44** £	**45**	**46** £	p
53	**54** £	**55**	**56** £	p

| | | | total of boxes 46 and 56 | |

63 Corporation tax   **63** £   p

64 Marginal rate relief   **64** £   p

65 Corporation tax net of marginal rate relief **65** £   p

66 Underlying rate of corporation tax   **66**   •   %

67 Profits matched with non-corporate distributions **67**

68 Tax at non-corporate distributions rate   **68** £   p

69 Tax at underlying rate on remaining profits **69** £   p

| | See note for box 70 in CT600 Guide |

70 Corporation tax chargeable   **70** £   p

CT600 (Short) (2008) Version 2

Task 9(a)

Analyse the following assets into those that are chargeable regarding CGT and those that are exempt.

✔

	Chargeable	Exempt
Disposals to connected persons		
Plant and machinery sold at a gain		
Cars		
Gifts to charities		

(b)

Response Limited bought a chattel in April 1998 for £4,000. The item was sold in April 2014 for £9,000, less sales commission of 5%.

The indexation factor from April 1998 to April 2014 is 0.573.

Complete the following table to calculate the chargeable gain.

	Amount £
Sale proceeds	
Sales commission	
Net sales proceeds	
Cost	
Indexation	
Provisional gain	
Chattel restriction	
Final gain	

Task 10

Bee Ltd bought 5,000 shares in Wye Ltd for £15,900 in October 2001. Bonus shares were issued in April 2002 at 1 for 10. A purchase of 2,000 shares was made on 20 April 2014 for £4.80 per share. On 25 April 2014 Bee Ltd sold 3,000 of the shares for £4.95 per share.

Indexation factors were:

October 2001 to April 2014: 0.467

Clearly showing the matching of the shares, calculate the gain or loss on the sale of shares and any pool balances remaining.

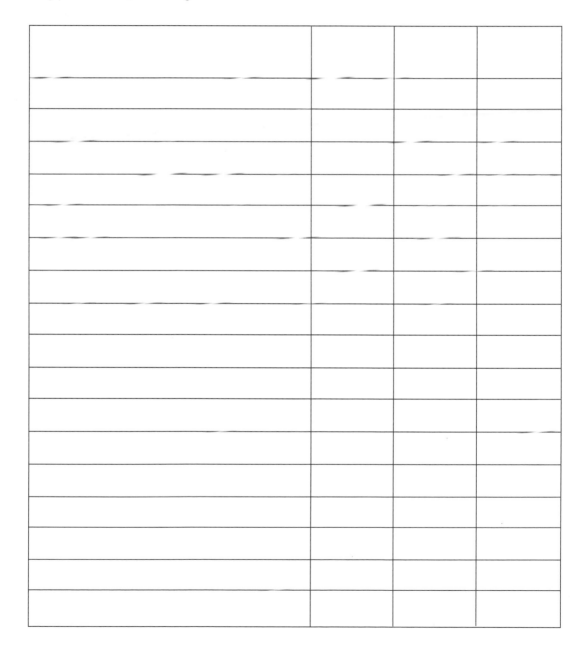

Task 11(a)

The following are the capital gains and losses made by Steve in 2013/14 and 2014/15. There were unused capital losses brought forward from 2012/13 totalling £3,000. The annual exempt amount is £10,900 in 2013/14 and £11,000 in 2014/15.

Year		£
2013/14	Gains	14,100
	Losses	6,300
2014/15	Gains	18,200
	Losses	1,400

Complete the following table, inserting zeros if appropriate.

	£
The amount of brought forward loss to be used in 2013/14	
The amount chargeable to CGT in 2013/14	
The amount of loss to be carried forward to 2014/15	
The amount chargeable to CGT in 2014/15	
The amount of loss to be carried forward to 2015/16	

(b)

Mary Poole is a sole trader who pays tax at the higher rate. She purchased a warehouse in October 2000 for £460,000, and sold it in September 2014 for £700,000. She then purchased a shop in December 2015 for £550,000.

(1)   Complete the following table relating to the gain on the sale of the warehouse, and deferral of that gain (if any). This was her only capital gain in 2014/15. Assume the gain does not qualify for entrepreneur's relief.

	£
Sale proceeds	
Cost	
Total gain	
Deferred gain	
Gain chargeable immediately	
Annual exempt amount	
Capital Gains Tax payable	

(2)   The cost of the shop will be deemed to be £ [   ] when it is ultimately sold.

Practice assessment 1 answers

Task 1

	£
Net profit per accounts	85,975
Add:	
Notional profit on goods for own use	750
Lesley's NIC and pension	8,125
Gifts of whisky	2,800
Costs of tax appeal	2,500
Private car expenses	1,950
Depreciation	22,680
	124,780
Less:	
Capital allowances	20,680
Adjusted profit	104,100

Task 2

CAP FOR THE 12 MONTHS TO 30/6/2014			
	Main Pool	**Special Rate Pool**	**Capital Allowances**
	£	£	£
WDV bf	105,000	17,000	
add			
Acquisitions with FYAs:			
Low emission car £25,000			
100% FYA £(25,000)			25,000
	0		
Acquisitions qualifying for AIA:			
Computer £290,000			
AIA claimed £(250,000)			250,000
Excess	40,000		
less			
Proceeds of Disposals	(5,000)		
	140,000	17,000	
WDA	(25,200)	(1,360)	26,560
WDV cf	114,800	15,640	
Total Capital Allowances			301,560

Maximum AIA is (£250,000 x 9/12) + (£500,000 x 3/12) = £312,500 but limited for purchases before 1/4/2014 to £250,000

Task 3(a)

(1)   The tax year in which she started trading was **2012/13**

(2)   Her taxable profits in her first tax year of trading were **£48,000**

(3)   Her taxable profits in her second tax year of trading were **£96,000**

(4)   Her taxable profits in her third tax year of trading were **£84,000**

(5)   Her overlap profits were **£24,000**

(b)

(1)

	Total	Ivor	Jo	Kirsty
	£	£	£	£
1 Jan – 31 July 2014	70,000	35,000	21,000	14,000
1 Aug – 31 Dec 2014	50,000	25,000	25,000	0
Total	120,000	60,000	46,000	14,000

(2)   The trading assessment for 2014/15 for Kirsty is **£14,000**

Task 4(a)

	CAP 12 months to 31/8/2014 £	CAP 4 months to 31/12/2014 £
Trading Profits before CAs	600,000	200,000
Capital Allowances	54,000	19,000
Trading Profits	546,000	181,000
Chargeable Gains	50,000	41,000
Rental Income	24,000	8,000
Sub total	620,000	230,000
Gift Aid	0	6,000
TTP	620,000	224,000

(b)

	£
Maximum of Band	250,000
Minimum of Band	50,000
Corporation Tax at Main Rate	29,400
Marginal Relief	275
Corporation Tax Payable	29,125

Task 5

(b), (d), (e) and (f) are correct

Task 6

(e) either £31,000 or £17,000 or nothing

Task 7

> The Corporation Tax Return (CT600) for the year ended 31 December 2013 should have been filed by 31 December 2014. The penalty for submitting over 3 months late is £200. If the return is now submitted promptly it should avoid a further penalty which could be imposed of 10% of the Corporation Tax (i.e. £4,500) for submissions over 6 months late.
>
> The final payment of Corporation Tax for the year ended 31 December 2013 should have been made by 1 October 2014. Interest will be payable (currently at 3%) from that date until payment is made. The company is not liable to make instalment payments, since based on the Corporation Tax amount that has been calculated, the company does not have taxable total profits over £1.5 million.
>
> There is a penalty for failing to keep appropriate records. This is up to £3,000 per chargeable accounting period. Provided the missing records only relate to 2013 then only one penalty of £3,000 may be charged.
>
> Looking forward, the tax return for the year ended 31 December 2014 should be filed by 31 December 2015, with the tax payment made by 1 October 2015.

Task 8

See completed form, opposite.

Task 9(a)

	Chargeable	Exempt
Government Stocks (gilts)		✔
Shares in Limited Companies	✔	
Trading Inventory		✔
Land	✔	

(b)

Proceeds: £7,100

Cost: £4,000

Indexation allowance: £2,000

Gain: £1,100

Chattel restriction on gain: £1,833

No. The chattel restriction will not limit the gain.

PARTNERSHIP STATEMENT (SHORT) *for the year ended 5 April 2014*

Please read these instructions before completing the Statement

Use these pages to allocate partnership income if the only income for the relevant return period was trading and professional income or taxed interest and alternative finance receipts from banks and building societies. Otherwise you must download or ask the SA Orderline for the *Partnership Statement (Full)* pages to record details of the allocation of all the partnership income. Go to hmrc.gov.uk/selfassessmentforms

Step 1 Fill in boxes 1 to 29 and boxes A and B as appropriate. Get the figures you need from the relevant boxes in the Partnership Tax Return. Complete a separate Statement for each accounting period covered by this Partnership Tax Return and for each trade or profession carried on by the partnership.

Step 2 Then allocate the amounts in boxes 11 to 29 attributable to each partner using the allocation columns on this page and page 7, read the Partnership Tax Return Guide, go to **hmrc.gov.uk/selfassessmentforms** If the partnership has more than three partners, please photocopy page 7.

Step 3 Each partner will need a copy of their allocation of income to fill in their personal tax return.

PARTNERSHIP INFORMATION

If the partnership business includes a trade or profession, enter here the accounting period for which appropriate items in this statement are returned.

Start **1** 1 / 4 / 14

End **2** 31 / 3 / 15

Nature of trade **3** Wholesale Fabric

MIXED PARTNERSHIPS

Tick here if this Statement is drawn up using Corporation Tax rules **4**

Tick here if this Statement is drawn up using tax rules for non-residents **5**

Individual partner details

6 Name of partner Alison Amsterdam

Address

Postcode

Date appointed as a partner
(if during 2012–13 or 2013–14)
7 /   /

Date ceased to be a partner
(if during 2012–13 or 2013–14)
9 /   /

Partner's Unique Taxpayer Reference (UTR)
8

Partner's National Insurance number
10

Partnership's profits, losses, income, tax credits, etc.

Tick this box if the items entered in the box had foreign tax taken off

Partner's share of profits, losses, income, tax credits, etc.

Copy figures in boxes 11 to 29 to boxes in the individual's **Partnership (short)** pages as shown below

• for an accounting period ended in 2013–14 ▼					
from box 3.83 Profit from a trade or profession **A**	**11** £ 80,000	Profit **11** £ 48,000	Copy this figure to box 8
from box 3.82 Adjustment on change of basis	**11A** £	**11A** £	Copy this figure to box 10
from box 3.84 Loss from a trade or profession **B**	**12** £	Loss **12** £	Copy this figure to box 8
from box 10.4 Business Premises Renovation Allowance	**12A** £	**12A** £	Copy this figure to box 15
• for the period 6 April 2013 to 5 April 2014*					
from box 7.9A UK taxed interest and taxed alternative finance receipts	**22** £ 2,000	**22** £ 1,200	Copy this figure to box 28
from box 3.97 CIS deductions made by contractors on account of tax	**24** £	**24** £	Copy this figure to box 30
from box 3.98 Other tax taken off trading income	**24A** £	**24A** £	Copy this figure to box 31
from box 7.8A Income Tax taken off	**25** £ 400	**25** £ 240	Copy this figure to box 29
from box 3.117 Partnership charges	**29** £	**29** £	Copy this figure to box 4, 'Other tax reliefs' section on page Ai 2 in your personal tax return

* if you are a 'CT Partnership' see the Partnership Tax Return Guide

SA800 2014   PARTNERSHIP TAX RETURN: PAGE 6

Task 10(a)

	No. Shares	Cost £	Indexed Cost £
Purchase October 2001	9,000	27,900	27,900
Bonus shares	900	0	0
Indexation to July 2003			3,181
Purchase July 2003	5,000	19,000	19,000
Sub total	14,900	46,900	50,081
Indexation to April 2014			20,533
Total	14,900	46,900	70,614
Disposal	(10,000)	(31,477)	(47,392)
Pool Balance	4,900	15,423	23,222

Proceeds	£50,000
Indexed Cost	£47,392
Gain	£2,608

(b)

(1)   The gain or loss on the sale of shares on 12 January 2015 is **£1,580 loss.**

(2)   The gain or loss on the sale of shares on 31 March 2015 is **£9,500 gain.**

Task 11(a)

	£
Sale proceeds	400,000
Cost	180,000
Total gain	220,000
Deferred gain	155,000
Gain chargeable immediately	65,000
Annual exempt amount	11,000
Capital Gains Tax payable	5,400

(b)

The cost of the shop will be deemed to be **£180,000** when it is ultimately sold.

Practice assessment 2 answers

Task 1(a)

	£
Profit	336,875
Disallowed items added back:	
Lisa's salary and personal pension contributions	75,400
Legal fees to purchase new office building	10,250
Operating lease of 180g/km car used for business	1,749
Expenses of Lisa's car which is used 70% for the business	3,750
Depreciation	155,310
Allowed items deducted:	
Capital allowances	21,380
Adjusted trading profits	561,954

(b)

	Add back to profit	Deduct from profit	No adjustment required
Loss on sale of non-current assets	✔		
Installation costs of new machinery	✔		
Discounts received for prompt payment			✔
Interest received on deposit account		✔	

Task 2

Period ended 31 December 2014	General pool £	Special rate pool £	Capital allowances £
WDV bf	157,500	31,680	
Additions FYA 29,500			
100% FYA (29,500)	0		29,500
Additions AIA			
Machinery 314,334			
AIA (£500,000 x 7/12) (291,667)			291,667
	22,667		
Sub totals	180,167	31,680	
WDA 18% x 7/12	(18,918)		18,918
WDA 8% x 7/12		(1,478)	1,478
WDV cf	161,249	30,202	
Capital Allowances			341,563
Period ended 30 April 2015			
WDV bf	161,249	30,202	
Disposal proceeds	(55,500)	(22,100)	
	(19,800)		
Balancing allowances	(85,949)	(8,102)	94,051
WDV cf	0	0	
Capital Allowances			94,051

Task 3

	Tax year	Basis period							Profit
	YYYY/YY	Day	Month	YYYY		Day	Month	YYYY	£
1st year	2012/13	1	Feb	2013	-	5	April	2013	19,600
2nd year	2013/14	1	Feb	2013	-	31	Jan	2014	121,500
3rd year	2014/15	1	Nov	2013	-	31	Oct	2014	133,200

The overlap profit is £52,900.

Task 4(a)

	First accounting period	**Second accounting period**
	£	£
Capital gains	5,510	19,475
Trading profits	113,556	47,315

(b)   TRUE

(c)

Data	£
Augmented profits	376,500
Maximum of relevant band	562,500

	£
Corporation tax at main rate	72,555
Marginal relief	427
Corporation tax payable	72,128

Marginal relief working:

1/400 x (£562,500 − £376,500) x (£345,500 / £376,500) = £427

Task 5

	Profits	**Class 4 at 9%**	**Class 4 at 2%**	**Total Class 4 NIC**
	£	£	£	£
Brian	49,280.00	3,051.81	148.30	3,200.11
Colin	40,320.00	2,912.76	0	2,912.76

Task 6

	£
How much trading loss can be claimed against income in the year ended 31 March 2015?	12,000
How much trading loss can be claimed against income in the year ended 31 March 2014?	29,250
How much trading loss can be carried forward to the year ended 31 March 2016?	0
How much capital loss can be carried forward against capital gains in the year ended 31 March 2016?	5,650
How much gift aid can be set against income in the year ended 31 March 2014?	1,800
How much gift aid can be set against income in the year ended 31 March 2015?	0
How much gift aid can be carried forward to be set against income in the year ended 31 March 2016?	0

Task 7

Companies that regularly pay Corporation Tax at the main rate without any marginal relief need to make payments on account before the normal final payment date. Craister Limited must be subject to these rules since its TTP is always above the band limit of £1.5 million.

Four payments on account are required, each based on one quarter of the estimated Corporation Tax for the CAP. The first payment on account is made on the 14th day of the 7th month of the CAP that it relates to. The next three payments follow at 3 month intervals. The final payment (based on any remaining actual liability) is made nine months and one day after the end of the CAP.

The following amounts will be payable after June 2015 by Craister Limited:

14 August 2015   £180,000 1st payment on account for y/e 31/1/16

(based on ¼ of estimated Corporation Tax of £720,000)

1 November 2015   £15,000 as final payment for y/e 31/1/15
(based on £935,000 minus estimate of £920,000)

14 November 2015   £180,000 2nd payment on account for y/e 31/1/16

14 February 2016   £180,000 3rd payment account for y/e 31/1/16

14 May 2016   £180,000 4th payment on account for y/e 31/1/16

The final payment for y/e 31/1/16 will be made on 1 November 2016.

Task 8

box 21 minus boxes 24, 30, 32 and 35		
37 Profits chargeable to corporation tax		**37** £ 1,635,000

Tax calculation

38 Franked investment income	**38** £ 30,000	
39 Number of associated companies in this period or	**39** 0	
40 Associated companies in the first financial year	**40**	
41 Associated companies in the second financial year	**41**	
42 Put an 'X' in box 42 if the company claims to be charged at the starting rate or the small companies' rate on any part of its profits, or is claiming marginal rate relief		**42**

Enter how much profit has to be charged and at what rate of tax

Financial year (yyyy)	Amount of profit	Rate of tax	Tax	
43 2 0 1 3	**44** £ 408,750	**45** 23%	**46** £ 94,012	p
53 2 0 1 4	**54** £ 1,226,250	**55** 21%	**56** £ 257,512	p
			total of boxes 46 and 56	
63 Corporation tax			**63** £ 351,524	p

Task 9(a)

	£	£
Proceeds		43,500
Disposal costs		300
Cost	19,850	
Buying costs	650	
Indexation allowance	10,250	
Gain		12,450

(b)

	True	False
Indexation allowance does not apply to individuals under CGT	✔	
A limited company can set an annual exempt amount against its gains		✔

Task 10

		Number of shares	Cost of shares £
April 1998	Purchase	3,000	9,000
July 2002	Bonus issue	1,000	0
		4,000	9,000
August 2003	Disposal	(800)	(1,800)
		3,200	7,200
January 2012	Purchase	5,000	23,200
		8,200	30,400
June 2014	Disposal	(2,500)	(9,268)
	Balance	5,700	21,132
	Proceeds	14,850	
	Cost	9,268	
	Gain	5,582	

Task 11

Taxpayer	Taxable income £	Gains chargeable at 18% £	Gains chargeable at 28% £	Total CGT payable £
Sonia	18,500	13,365	10,635	5,383
Steve	41,250	0	24,000	6,720

Practice assessment 3 answers

Task 1(a)

	Add back to net profit	Deduct from net profit	No adjustment required
Bank interest receivable		✔	
Bank interest payable			✔
Increase in general provision for irrecoverable debts	✔		
Profit on sale of non-current assets		✔	
Staff travelling expenses			✔
Owner's class 2 & 4 NIC	✔		
Discounts receivable			✔

(b)

	£
Profit	400,180
Disallowed items added back:	
Operating lease of 180g/km car	1,479
Replacement of office furniture	12,000
Depreciation	245,110
Allowed items deducted:	
Capital allowances	33,780
Adjusted trading profits	624,989

Task 2

	Main pool	Special rate pool	Capital allowances
	£	£	£
WDV bf	125,000	47,000	
Additions without FYA or AIA:			
Car		28,000	
Additions qualifying for AIA:			
Computer system			
325,833			
AIA* (187,500)			187,500
	138,333		
Disposals	(5,000)		
	258,333	75,000	
WDA 18% x 8/12	(31,000)		31,000
WDA 8% x 8/12		(4,000)	4,000
WDV cf	227,333	71,000	
Total Capital Allowances			222,500

* Maximum AIA: (£250,000 x 7/12) + (£500,000 x 1/12) = £187,500

Task 3(a)

	Tax year	Amount £
First year of trading	2012/13	17,000
Second year of trading[1]	2013/14	100,500
Third year of trading	2014/15	84,000
Overlap profits[2]		24,000

(1) 1/2/13-31/1/14 £93,500 + (£84,000 x 1/12) = £100,500

(2) (1/2/13-5/4/13) + (1/1/14-31/1/14) = (£17,000 + £7,000) = £24,000

Task 3(b)

(1)

	Total	Adam	Ben	Clive	Catherine
	£	£	£	£	£
Period to 31 May	150,000	75,000	45,000	30,000	0
Period from 1 June	210,000	70,000	70,000	0	70,000
Total	360,000	145,000	115,000	30,000	70,000

(2)

	Assessable profits £
Adam	145,000
Ben	115,000
Clive	30,000
Catherine	103,000

Note: Catherine's assessable profits are based on the period 1 June 2014 – 5 April 2015:
£70,000 + (£396,000 / 3 x 3/12) = £103,000

Task 4(a)

	CAP 12 months to 31/7/2014	CAP 5 months to 31/12/2014
	£	£
Trading Profits before CAs	504,000	210,000
Capital Allowances	74,000	41,000
Trading Profits	430,000	169,000
Chargeable Gains	0	6,000
Rental Income	37,200	15,500
Sub total	467,200	190,500
Gift Aid	0	6,000
TTP	467,200	184,500

(b)

	Financial Year 2013	Financial Year 2014	Total
	£	£	£
Corporation Tax at Full Rate	72,450	198,450	
Marginal Relief	65	65	
Corporation Tax Payable	72,385	198,385	270,770

Task 5

(a) and (d) are TRUE; (b) and (c) are FALSE.

Task 6

	2013	2014	2015
	£	£	£
Trading profits	120,500	0	375,000
Trading loss offset against trading profits only	0	0	0
Net chargeable gains	50,300	0	0
Rental income	10,800	12,400	14,200
Trading loss offset against taxable total profits	72,600	12,400	0
Taxable total profits after offsetting losses	109,000	0	389,200

Task 7

Explanation of amounts payable

On 31 January 2016 the final payment for 2014/15 will be due for income tax. This will be calculated as:

Income tax for 2014/15	£31,630
Less already paid on account (2 x £11,900)	£23,800
Balancing payment for 2014/15	£7,830

In addition a payment on account for 2015/16 will be due at the same time. This is based on 50% of the total income tax for 2014/15 of £31,630 – i.e £15,815.

The total payable on 31 January 2016 will therefore be:

Balancing payment for 2014/15	£7,830
First payment on account for 2015/16	£15,815
	£23,645

A second payment on account for 2015/16 of £15,815 will be due on 31 July 2016.

Implications of not making payments when due

Interest will be due on all late payments. The interest rate is currently 3% pa.

In addition, penalties are payable for late payment of the balancing payment for a tax year (not on payments on account). If a balancing payment is between 30 days and 6 months late the penalty would be 5% of the tax.

In this case it would therefore be 5% x £7,830 = £392.

If the payment was over 6 months late there would be a further 5% penalty, and another 5% if over 12 months late.

Task 8

Company tax calculation

Turnover

1	Total turnover from trade or profession	**1**	£

Income

3	Trading and professional profits	**3** £ 1,830,000	
4	Trading losses brought forward claimed against profits	**4** £ 130,000	
		box 3 minus box 4	
5	Net trading and professional profits	**5** £ 1,700,000	
6	Bank, building society or other interest, and profits and gains from non-trading loan relationships	**6** £	
11	Income from UK land and buildings	**11** £ 110,000	
14	Annual profits and gains not falling under any other heading	**14** £	

Chargeable gains

16	Gross chargeable gains	**16** £ 89,000	
17	Allowable losses including losses brought forward	**17** £ 13,000	
		box 16 minus box 17	
18	Net chargeable gains	**18** £ 76,000	
		sum of boxes 5, 6, 11, 14 & 18	
21	**Profits before other deductions and reliefs**	**21** £ 1,886,000	

Deductions and Reliefs

24	Management expenses under S75 ICTA 1988	**24** £	
30	Trading losses of this or a later accounting period under S393A ICTA 1988	**30** £	
31	Put an 'X' in box 31 if amounts carried back from later accounting periods are included in box 30	**31**	
32	Non-trade capital allowances	**32** £	
35	Charges paid	**35** £ 40,000	
		box 21 minus boxes 24, 30, 32 and 35	
37	**Profits chargeable to corporation tax**	**37** £ 1,846,000	

Tax calculation

38	Franked investment income	**38** £	
39	Number of associated companies in this period or	**39** 0	
40	Associated companies in the first financial year	**40**	
41	Associated companies in the second financial year	**41**	
42	Put an 'X' in box 42 if the company claims to be charged at the starting rate or the small companies' rate on any part of its profits, or is claiming marginal rate relief	**42**	

Enter how much profit has to be charged and at what rate of tax

Financial year (yyyy)	Amount of profit	Rate of tax	Tax	
43 2 0 1 4	**44** £ 1,846,000	**45** 21%	**46** £ 387,660	p
53	**54** £	**55**	**56** £	p
			total of boxes 46 and 56	
63 Corporation tax			**63** £ 387,660	p

64	Marginal rate relief	**64** £	p
65	Corporation tax net of marginal rate relief	**65** £ 387,660	p
66	Underlying rate of corporation tax	**66** 21•00 %	
67	Profits matched with non-corporate distributions	**67**	
68	Tax at non-corporate distributions rate	**68** £	p
69	Tax at underlying rate on remaining profits	**69** £	p
		See note for box 70 in CT600 Guide	
70	**Corporation tax chargeable**	**70** £ 387,660	p

Task 9(a)

	Chargeable	Exempt
Disposals to connected persons	✔	
Plant and machinery sold at a gain	✔	
Cars		✔
Gifts to charities		✔

(b)

	Amount £
Sale proceeds	9,000
Sales commission	450
Net sales proceeds	8,550
Cost	4,000
Indexation	2,292
Provisional gain	2,258
Chattel restriction	5,000
Final gain	2,258

Task 10

Matching shares bought 20 April 2014	£		
Proceeds (2,000)	9,900		
Cost	9,600		
Gain	300		
Share pool	No	£	£
October 2001 purchase	5,000	15,900	15,900
Bonus shares	500		
Indexation			7,425
Sub total	5,500	15,900	23,325
Disposal	(1,000)	(2,891)	(4,241)
Pool balance	4,500	13,009	19,084
Matching with pool	£		
Proceeds (1,000)	4,950		
Indexed cost	4,241		
Gain	709		
Total gain	1,009		

Task 11(a)

	£
The amount of brought forward loss to be used in 2013/14	0
The amount chargeable to CGT in 2013/14	0
The amount of loss to be carried forward to 2014/15	3,000
The amount chargeable to CGT in 2014/15	2,800
The amount of loss to be carried forward to 2015/16	0

The loss brought forward from 2012/13 of £3,000 is not used in 2013/14 since the net gains that year are already below the annual exemption.

(b)

(1)

	£
Sale proceeds	700,000
Cost	460,000
Total gain	240,000
Deferred gain	90,000
Gain chargeable immediately	150,000
Annual exempt amount	11,000
Capital Gains Tax payable	38,920

(2)   The cost of the shop will be deemed to be **£460,000** when it is ultimately sold.

for your notes

for your notes

for your notes

for your notes

for your notes

_____